Unshakable Kingdom

A Fresh Look at Hebrews

James J. Burke

Fireproof Commentaries

Volume III

FIREPROOF
COMMENTARIES

ISBN-13: — 979-8-9941637-2-6

All Scripture quotations are taken from the King
James Version of the Bible unless otherwise
indicated.

Printed in the United States of America
fireproofcommentaries.org

To Roxanne—

For your steadfast love and quiet strength in every storm.

She's beautiful,
As she whispers to me
Whispers words just for me
When I'm tired
and worn
And weary at heart
She whispers reminders, "It's ok."
"HE knows." "Just keep going".
She's my strength
And she's beautiful.

Preface

The letter to the Hebrews is not an easy read. It stretches our minds with priestly language, temple imagery, and the steady weight of Old Testament resonance. Yet within those layers lies one of Scripture's clearest portraits of Jesus Christ—the One who not only speaks for God but is God's final Word. Hebrews calls us to endurance, not escape; to maturity, not emotion; to worship that holds steady when the earth itself trembles.

This volume, Unshakable Kingdom, is the third in the Fireproof Commentaries series. It continues the same pattern of exposition, summary, application, and prayer, built for personal study, small groups, and churches that desire depth without losing devotion. The aim is the same as always: to build lives that withstand the fire.

While the first two volumes—*Building a Fireproof Church* and *Colony of Heaven*—looked at the church's foundation and identity, Hebrews turns our eyes upward to the finishing work of Christ, our Priest and King. Every page declares that the believer's security rests not in circumstance but in the seated Savior who cannot be moved.

The sermons that shaped these pages were preached to a small congregation that loves the Word and listens patiently as their pastor thinks aloud in Scripture. What grew from those sermons became this book: a journey through the text that prays, teaches, and occasionally trembles before the majesty of Christ.

My prayer is that this study will renew your confidence in the sufficiency of Jesus. The same hands that shaped creation now hold you fast; the same voice that spoke in fragments now speaks in fullness. May your faith find footing in that Unshakable Kingdom which cannot be moved.

— James J. Burke

Marinette, Wisconsin

2025

Table of Contents

Introduction: The Unshakable Kingdom—A Fresh Look at Hebrews

Hebrews stands apart in the New Testament—no named sender, no direct address, just a rush of revelation centered on the Son. This sparseness leaves room for inference, especially as to its audience, but the clues build a clear picture. We will trace the basics: authorship, form, timing, and recipients. Then we will linger on that community, unpacking the three types of hearers it implies—a key lens for the letter's tougher stretches. From there, the revelation's sweep and anchoring themes set the stage for the chapters ahead. My goal is to stir understanding that strengthens obedience, whether in personal quiet time, small group discussion, or church-wide teaching. Each chapter moves from exposition to summary insights from the series, then to everyday application, closing with prayer.

The Unknown Author: Focus on the Message

Hebrews opens without a byline, thrusting readers into God's final word through his Son (Heb 1:1–2). This isn't carelessness; it spotlights Christ over any human source. Early writers tied it to Paul—Clement of Alexandria saw him writing in Hebrew, with Luke translating to Greek; Origen noted the ideas match Paul's theology, though the style differs, concluding only God truly knows the human pen. The Eastern church favored this view, drawn to the Pauline passion for Old Testament fulfillment in Jesus.

Scholars today highlight the variances: the Greek runs smoother than Paul's, with less emphasis on grace as a repeated theme and more on priestly order. Suggestions include Apollos, the eloquent teacher from Acts 18 whose background fits the rhetorical flair; Barnabas, a Levite whose heritage aligns with the temple imagery; or Priscilla, a key instructor whose name might have been omitted for cultural reasons. Paul's influence persists in the scriptural depth and Christ-exalting drive. Many see it as his last dissertation, dictated from prison and refined by a scribe. For this study, the exact hand matters less than the content: a charge to see Jesus as supreme, freeing us to hear without distraction.

A Spoken Word: Sermon Form for Exhortation

The letter reads more like a preached message than private mail—rhythmic, with teaching blocks flowing into urgent calls to action. It ends as a "word of exhortation" (Heb 13:22), echoing synagogue invitations for homilies (Acts 13:15). Likely delivered orally first, perhaps in a Jewish-Christian gathering, then circulated in writing. The style blends exposition with midrash-like interpretation, polished Greek laced with over thirty Old Testament quotations and fifty allusions. Chapter 1 alone stacks seven to prove the Son's glory outshines angels.

This form fits its aim: not abstract study, but communal urging to "hold fast" (Heb 3:6). In our fragmented reading habits, it pulls us back to hearing Scripture together, where truth moves from head to hands.

Written on History's Edge: Mid-60s Timing

Clues date it to the 60s AD, before Jerusalem's temple fell in AD 70. References to ongoing sacrifices (Heb 8:4–5; 9:6–9; 10:1–4) assume the old system still operates, untouched by that destruction. Persecution echoes Nero's era (Heb 10:32–34), and the faith comes secondhand from eyewitnesses (Heb

2:3), placing it after AD 60 but before the cataclysm—likely 64–69 AD. If Pauline, it marks his prison finale, full of unbowed zeal.

This timing sharpens the message: as old structures cracked, the letter points from shadows to substance —Christ's offering that ends all others. The exhortation to turn from the shadow to the Reality would have prepared the hearers for the destruction of the temple, allowing them to retain their faith when their cultural foundation was swept away. It equips readers then and now to release what fades for what endures.

The Community: Jewish Believers and the Three Types of Hearers

Hebrews addresses no specific church like Corinth or Rome, just "brothers" in a general call (Heb 3:12; 13:22–25). The tone and content point to Jewish Christians, likely in Asia or Palestine—steeped in temple practices, facing synagogue exclusion and Roman suspicion. They know the law's rhythms but hear Jesus as its fulfillment, with warnings against reverting to old ways (Heb 13:9).

A vital inference emerges here: the community holds three kinds of hearers, mixed in one assembly. This isn't explicitly addressed in the text, but can be clearly seen in a careful reading of the text's various appeals

—exhortations to the committed, invitations to the curious, rebukes to the hesitant. It's an inference, drawn from patterns in the warnings and encouragements, much like Paul's layered address to Corinth's factions or Ephesus' diverse walks. Why does it hold? The letter shifts tones without clear breaks: bold affirmations of access to God (Heb 4:16; 10:19–22) suit the faithful; reminders of Jesus' signs and superiority (Heb 2:1–4) draw the intrigued; stark threats of judgment (Heb 6:4–8; 10:26–31) jolt the resistant. These aren't blanket condemnations but targeted words, assuming a spectrum in the room. Scholars like deSilva and Lane note this rhetorical strategy, common in Jewish homilies, to address a real group's dynamics without alienating any (deSilva 2000, 234–36; Lane 1991, 142–44).

This lens unlocks the difficult passages. Take Hebrews 6:4–6: those "enlightened" who "tasted the heavenly gift" yet fall away—it's not a final verdict on all believers but a sobering push for holdouts who've sampled grace without surrender, urging them back before roots wither. Or Hebrews 10:26–31: willful sin after truth's knowledge warns resisters against trampling Christ's blood, while bolstering the faithful with covenant security (v. 23). The intrigued get the bridge: partial taste invites full commitment. Without this threefold view, the warnings risk scaring off the steady or confusing the seeking. With it, they become pastoral triage—strengthening, summoning, shaking

5

as needed. This frees us to see the text's mercy: God speaks to every seat in the house, pulling all toward the Unshakable Kingdom.

We've known these types in our own circles—the anchored who lead quietly; the admirers who affirm from afar; the lingerers who nod but don't yield. Spotting them in Hebrews turns its edges into empathy, equipping us to extend the same grace in our churches today.

Revelation's Fullness: From Partial to Final in the Son

The letter launches the history of Divine revelation: partial through prophets and fathers (Heb 1:1), complete in these last days by the Son (Heb 1:2). From creation's call to cross's consummation, it traces the arc—law's shadow yielding to gospel's light. No more fragments; Jesus embodies the Father, securing redemption that awaits his return. This positions the church as outpost holders: no fallback, just faithful advance in a resistant age.

Anchoring Themes: Christ as Better and Final

Hebrews builds on superiority: Son over angels (chs. 1–2), Moses (ch. 3), priests (chs. 4–7), Old Covenant (chs. 8–10). Faith's examples cheer us (ch. 11), discipline refines (chs. 12–13). Key anchors—finished atonement (Heb 9:26–28), true rest (Heb 4:9–11), piercing Word (Heb 4:12)—lead to the kingdom received with thanks and awe (Heb 12:28) (Enter the Bible 2025; Bible Hub 2025). The refrain? Consider Jesus (Heb 3:1; 12:2)—our superior priest, eternal hope.

In days that tremble, Hebrews steadies the soul—not with dreams of escape, but with the strength to live out the Kingdom that will not be shaken.

1

God Has Spoken: The Son's Full Revelation (Hebrews 1:1–4)

Hebrews bursts open not with a formal greeting or doctrinal outline, but with a poetic proclamation—a hymn-like declaration of God's speaking voice through the ages, culminating in the Son. This isn't mere prologue; it's the letter's thesis, thrusting us into the heart of revelation's drama.

"God, who at sundry times and in divers manners spake in time past unto the fathers by the prophets, Hath in these last days spoken unto us by his Son, whom he hath appointed heir of all things, by whom also he made the worlds; Who being the brightness of his glory, and the express image of his person, and upholding all things by the word of his power, when he had by himself purged our sins, sat

*down on the right hand of the Majesty on high;
Being made so much better than the angels, as
he hath by inheritance obtained a more
excellent name than they" (Heb. 1:1–4).*

Here, the author sets the stage for Christ's
supremacy, urging a mixed community of hearers to
heed the final, full Word amid fading shadows. This
passage grips us as dawn breaking over history's
epochs: partial glimpses yielding to the Son's blaze,
freeing us from fruitless chasing after *more*. For
believers, it's an anchor; for admirers, an invitation; for
resisters, a reckoning. As scholar James W.
Thompson notes, this "centerpiece of the author's
persuasive effort" claims God's ultimate disclosure in
a Son, over against the incomplete prophetic past,
demanding our undivided gaze.

This opening not only introduces Hebrews'
Christology but structures its entire argument,
alternating exposition and exhortation to press us
forward into unshakable faith. The poem's progressive
contrast—past fragments to eschatological fullness—
unfolds God's redemptive history, preparing the
community for trials like synagogue exclusion or
Nero's persecution (Heb. 10:32–34). In a world of
half-truths and self-revelations, it calls us to the Son's
sufficiency, where theology meets trembling hearts.
We'll unpack the poem's layers, draw from the

sermon's fire, apply its edge to each class of hearer, a message for the follower, the admirer and the rejector.

The Poem of Revelation

Hebrews 1:1–4 forms a majestic progressive statement, a "Christological kernel" that encapsulates the book's themes of superiority and sonship. Far from a casual introduction, it's a rhetorical trumpet, blending Hellenistic hymnody with Jewish midrash to exalt the Son as God's climactic Word. The book's structure hums with a simple rhythm: it starts with a big claim right up front (in verses 1–4), then unpacks it step by step through deep teaching

> **Midrash**
>
> A traditional Jewish method of interpreting Scripture that seeks meaning beyond the literal text. *Midrash* often expands, explains, or applies biblical passages through stories, analogies, and moral insights.

(from 1:5 all the way to 10:18), and wraps up by calling us to live it out with fresh energy (10:19–13:21). You'll spot this flow in those repeated Greek phrases like "so much better" (at 1:4 and 10:25), which hammer home how superior Christ is in every way. It's like the whole letter follows a heartbeat— here's the truth (cause), now run with it (response)— turning head knowledge into everyday grit, just as it calls itself a "word of exhortation" (13:22) to build lasting faith.

While most translations obscure its poetry, the rhythm emerges in line breaks that echo ancient hymns, perhaps echoing Philippians 2:6–11 or Colossians 1:15–20. Here is my own poetic but accurate translation:

In many portions and many ways
In Ancient Past
God has spoken to the Fathers
Through the Prophets.
Upon the Last of the Days
He spoke to us in the Son
Who He established The Inheritor of All;
Through Whom He Performed the Ages;
Who exists as
The Dawning of His Glory
And the Expression of His Essence;
Who carries forth everything
By His mighty word
Having worked purification of sins
Sat down on the right hand
Of the Exalted Majesty
Becoming far greater than
The angels,
He has inherited an Exalted Name.

Verse 1 surveys antiquity with a sweeping overview at God's progressive self-disclosure: "God, who at sundry times and in divers manners spake in time past unto the fathers by the prophets" (Heb. 1:1). The Greek phrase *polymeros kai polytropos*—literally "in many parts and in many ways"—captures the piecemeal, multifaceted nature of this revelation, like shards of a mosaic slowly forming a larger picture. It wasn't a single, overwhelming download but a deliberate unfolding, varied in form (visions, laws, whispers, signs) and timed for response, demanding step-by-step obedience from those who heard. As Ellingworth observes, this "designed incompleteness" ensured each fragment tested the heart, building obedience as the foundation for what followed (Ellingworth 1993, 93). God never handed over the full scroll at once; He doled it out in portions, expecting us to live the known before unveiling more —like a father teaching a child to walk before running. This era of antiquity, spanning Creation to Christ, reveals a God who persists in speaking to a rebellious creation, each disclosure layering grace upon judgment, promise upon warning, and always pointing forward to the ultimate Word yet to come.

Consider the dawn of revelation in Genesis, where the voice of God breaks the silence of creation with intimacy and purpose. All that exists springs forth by His word—except man. Humanity is fashioned by His hands and animated by His breath (Gen. 2:7), a union of dust and divinity, created to bear His image and represent His rule over the earth. From a world already called very good (Gen. 1:31), God gathered the best and planted a garden for His beloved creature, filling it with abundance and companionship. In its midst, He placed two trees—symbols of His own heart. The Tree of Life stood as a perpetual offer of immortality: eternal fellowship with the Giver of Life. The Tree of the Knowledge of Good and Evil stood as the solemn reminder that love must be chosen. For love without choice is not love at all.

Man already knew good—he walked with Goodness Himself. But the serpent whispered that there was more to know, that independence was enlightenment, that rebellion was wisdom. Eve desired to experience what life might be apart from God; Adam, loving his wife more than his Maker, joined her. They ate, and their eyes were opened—not to glory, but to guilt. They saw what evil looked like from the inside. Shame, fear, and mistrust entered the world with them. The first family fractured before the first child was born.

And yet, God did not storm away from His creation. He came walking still, not in rage but in sorrow. His curse was not vindictive but consequential—"cursed is the ground for thy sake" (Gen. 3:17). The phrase could be read, "for your benefit." God allowed the earth to bear thorns that man might taste what he had chosen: life on his own terms. The world's brokenness is not evidence of God's cruelty but of His honesty. Every pain, every loss, every evil we encounter is the echo of that ancient choice—to know evil rather than to trust good.

Yet even in judgment, grace spoke. God clothed their shame with the skin of sacrifice, whispering a promise that a Deliverer would come—the woman's seed who would crush the serpent's head (Gen. 3:15, 21). The first prophecy was not addressed to man, for man still imagined adventure in his rebellion. He left the garden not in despair but in defiance. And still, God's mercy followed him. Blood was spilled before man ever built an altar, that he might learn the cost of sin and the certainty of redemption. From that moment on, every shadow of evil points us back to the goodness of God, who even through our defiance was already preparing the cross.

The pattern deepens with Cain, where revelation shifts to corrective clarity, underscoring God's holiness in worship. After Abel's blood-offering pleases while Cain's work does not, God doesn't strike but warns: "Why art thou wroth? ... If thou doest well, shalt thou not be accepted? And if thou doest not well, sin lieth at the door" (Gen. 4:6–7). This portion reveals a God who instructs in righteousness, valuing heart-obedience over ritual form (cf. 1 Sam. 15:22). Cain hears, but rejects—his way trumps God's, birthing murder and exile, his blood-cry echoing Abel's (Gen. 4:8–10). Like Adam's grab for control, Cain's defiance amplifies the curse, turning soil to blood-soaked wanderer's waste (Gen. 4:11–12). Yet even here, God marks him for protection (Gen. 4:15), layering grace atop warning: revelation as lifeline, not lash. How many times do we say, "Well, I think my way works better"? These early revelations test surrender, building a trajectory from provision's gift to correction's call, each rebellion deepening humanity's ache while heightening the need for a fuller Word.

Grace's thread thickens in Noah's day, where revelation expands to redemptive rescue amid universal rot. As corruption floods the earth (Gen. 6:5, 11–12), God speaks judgment yet singles out Noah: "Noah found grace in the eyes of the Lord" (Gen. 6:8), commanding ark-building as covenant-sign (Gen. 6:13–22). This portion unveils God as just—dealing with sin, yet gracious—rainbow-sealed promise never to drown creation again (Gen. 9:11–17). Noah obeys —600 years hammering gopher wood—modeling fidelity that saves humanity and all the animals (Gen. 7:1; Heb. 11:7). But post-flood, the build falters: Noah's vineyard lapse (Gen. 9:20–21) echoes Eden's fall, Ham's dishonor cursing generations (Gen. 9:22–25). Revelation here layers ark-grace upon garden-provision and Cain-correction: from intimate walk to global wash, God's voice preserves a remnant, but human frailty persists, pointing to a deeper cleansing beyond wood and water is needed.

The story of revelation steadies and deepens with Abraham. When humanity again forgets its Maker, God speaks into the noise of idolatry with a call that sounds both simple and staggering: "Get thee out... and I will make of thee a great nation" (Gen. 12:1–3). One man, surrounded by pagan altars, is summoned to trust an unseen land and an untested promise. God binds Himself to that promise with covenant—His word sealed by His own name. What began in Eden's garden now moves toward a people, a lineage, a plan of redemption that cannot fail.

Years later, the same God leads Abraham to Moriah's height, the knife trembling in his hand. It is here that promise and obedience collide. "By Myself have I sworn," the Lord declares, "that in blessing I will bless thee" (Gen. 22:16–18). The ram caught in the thicket becomes the emblem of substitution, and Abraham learns that covenant love demands costly faith but always provides gracious provision. Revelation matures from mere hearing to holy proving; faith becomes not belief alone, but surrender.

From Abraham's altar to Moses' mountain, the covenant widens and clarifies. The God who swore by Himself now thunders from Sinai, inscribing His holiness in stone. Promise gives birth to precept, and the scattered family becomes a nation. Yet the pattern remains unchanged: man falters, God remains faithful. The line bends through Ishmael's impatience and Esau's disdain, but it never breaks. Every failure becomes a footnote to divine fidelity.

Then revelation moves from covenant to conscience, from mountain to message. Through prophets and psalms, the divine voice grows more personal, even as the nation grows more wayward. The same God who thundered at Sinai now speaks in song and sorrow. Through David's harp, He reveals the Shepherd's heart; through Isaiah's lament, the suffering Servant; through Jeremiah's tears, the wounded Lover who will not forsake His bride. Each prophet becomes a window, and through each window more light breaks in—grace filtered through judgment, hope glowing through ruin.

The covenant people hear, but seldom heed. Altars rise beside idols; kings forget their calling; priests grow proud while widows starve. Yet still the word comes—relentless, merciful, unyielding. "What could have been done more to My vineyard?" God asks (Isa. 5:4). Revelation presses forward not because man deserves it, but because God refuses to abandon His plan. Each failure only magnifies His patience; each generation becomes another canvas for mercy's persistence. These ancient day glimpses were preparatory scaffolding—authoritative, yes, but incomplete, like stars wheeling toward sunrise.

Portions built progressively: provision tested loyalty (Adam), correction clarified worship (Cain), grace preserved remnant (Noah), oath forged family (Abraham), law structured nation (Moses), prophets previewed renewal (Isaiah et al.). Each layer exposed frailty—rebellion's ripple from garden to exile—yet layered mercy deeper, God's broken heart threading through (Gen. 6:6; Hos. 11:8). Spurned, they birthed our shadowed world (Rom. 5:12); heeded, they hinted at unshakable dawn. Just as on a clear morning you begin to see a glow in the east, prophets glowing of something better, something coming, building relentlessly to the Last Days' blaze in the Son.

Verse 2 marks a dramatic turn in the poem, swinging us from the scattered whispers of the past straight into the bold, complete shout of the present. "Hath in these last days spoken unto us by his Son" (Heb. 1:2a)—it's like the author flips a switch, lighting up everything that came before. No more tip-toeing around hints or half-stories; this is the arrival we've been waiting for. The phrase "these last days" carries a weight that's easy to miss in our fast-forward world, but it packs a punch. In Greek, it's *ep' eschatou tōn hēmerōn toutōn*, which literally means "upon the last of these days." It's not talking about some distant doomsday clock ticking down to the end of everything. Instead, it points to a shift that's already happened—a new chapter in God's big story that kicked off at the cross.

The Old Testament prophets talked a lot about the "day of the Lord," that big moment when God would step in to judge sin and set things right (Isa. 2:12; Joel 2:1). But here's the twist—when Peter stands up on Pentecost and quotes Joel, he says that day started with Jesus' coming, the pouring out of the Holy Spirit, and the whole messianic push forward (Acts 2:17). The cross was the spark: sin judged once for all, grace flooding out like dawn chasing night. This "last days" age stretches from Calvary all the way to Jesus' return—what we call the *Parousia* (Heb. 9:26; 10:37). It's the era where the old shadows start melting away, and the full light of God's plan takes over. We might call it the "now-age"—not a waiting room for heaven, but the final stretch where God's giving humanity one last, clear shot at surrender. No more previews; this is the main event, running from the empty tomb to the final trumpet.

> **Parousia**
>
> A Greek term meaning *presence* or *coming*, used in the New Testament for Christ's return in glory at the end of the age.

What makes this pivot so electric is how it ends the old installments for good. Up till now, God's been handing out revelation like chapters in a book you read one at a time—enough to get the gist, but leaving you hungry for the next page. The prophets gave glimpses: a suffering servant here (Isa. 53), a new heart there (Jer. 31:33), bones rattling back to life somewhere else (Ezek. 37). Each one built on the last, testing if we'd obey the bit we had before getting more. But verse 2 says, "Enough previews—the Son is here." That little phrase "by his Son" isn't just a tool in God's toolbox; it's qualitative, meaning the revelation **is** the Son Himself. He's not delivering a message like a mailman; He **is** the message, God's very essence wrapped in skin and walking among us (John 1:14; 14:9). the Father's heart and character finally voiced in a way we can touch, hear, and follow.

Back in the garden, God walked and talked face-to-face, but sin slammed the door. With Cain, it was a quiet warning over a botched offering. Noah got blueprints for a boat in a drowning world. Abraham heard promises under starlit skies, Moses received tablets on a smoking mountain—the prophets wrapped it all in visions of hope and heartbreak. Each time, it was real, but partial—like stars twinkling before sunrise, beautiful but not the full warmth you need to start your day. Jesus isn't an add-on or upgrade; He's the point, the flesh-and-blood clarity that makes the old words come alive. As He told Philip, "He that hath seen me hath seen the Father" (John 14:9). No more guessing; in the Son, we see love that stoops to our mess, wrath that burns clean at the cross, and grace that raises us new.

This shift isn't just ancient history—it's our story too. We're living in these "last days," right smack in the middle of God's final act. The cross didn't wrap things up; it launched the countdown, where the church stands as His embassy in a world still saying no. There is no Plan B if we fumble. The Son's arrival means the portions are over—obey what is true today, because tomorrow is not promised another hint. For that Jewish community hearing this Hebrews sermon for the first time, facing synagogue cold shoulders and Roman heat, it was a lifeline: don't cling to fading rituals; the real temple, the true sacrifice, walked Galilee and hung on Golgotha. For us? Same truth. In a culture chasing "fresh revelations" on every screen, this poem whispers (and shouts): You've got the full download in Jesus. Why scroll for scraps when the Author's here?

All those fragments—the garden's innocence, the covenant's oath, the law's thunder, the prophet's cry— gather their meaning in Him. The Word that once came through men now comes as Man. Where every earlier voice faded into echo, His endures. The Father who once spoke in portions has now spoken in Person (Heb. 1:1–2). In Christ, revelation finds its rest. The shadow yields to substance, the promise to Presence, the yearning to fulfillment.

No longer must man strain to hear through veils of law or longing; the Word walks among us. The same breath that animated Adam now speaks peace to storms and life to tombs. The age of fragments has closed, and the age of fullness has begun. To live in these last days, then, is not to count down toward an ending, but to dwell already in completion—to see every Scripture, every story, every sorrow converge in the Son who holds all things by the word of His power.

Next we listen as the Son's sevenfold portrait cascades, each clause a jewel in supremacy's crown:

Heir of All Things (v. 2a): The poem doesn't stop at the Son's arrival—it dives right into who He is, starting with His royal status: "whom he hath appointed heir of all things" (Heb. 1:2b). In Greek, that's hon *ethēken klēronomon pantōn*—God has officially named Him the heir, the one set to rule it all. This isn't some casual family hand-me-down; it's a king's decree, echoing the ancient royal promise in Psalm 2: "Ask of me, and I shall give thee the heathen for thine inheritance, and the uttermost parts of the earth for thy possession" (Ps. 2:8). Picture David on his throne, but zoomed out to cosmic scale—the Father crowning the Son as rightful ruler over every inch of creation, from distant galaxies to the dirt under our feet. Back in the Old Testament, this "royal bequest" was God's vow to His anointed king, a son who would smash rebels and claim the world as prize (Ps. 2:7–8). Now, Hebrews says it's Jesus—declared at His baptism ("Thou art my beloved Son"; Mark 1:11), sealed at resurrection ("Declared to be the Son of God with power"; Rom. 1:4).

But here lies the beautiful tension: the inheritance is His by right, yet not in full possession. The will stands signed and sealed, unbreakable in heaven's court, but its transfer unfolds in time. The Son now sits at the Father's right hand, waiting until "His enemies be made His footstool" (Ps. 110:1; Heb. 10:13). The picture is regal and patient—the Conqueror enthroned beside His Father, the victory complete though the final unveiling still to come. Every knee will bow, every tongue will confess (Phil. 2:10–11), but until that day, the clock of mercy still runs—justice ripening, rebels invited to repent, and the Bride being readied for the Kingdom's full dawn.

This waiting isn't wasted time; it's our growing season. As co-heirs—"joint-heirs with Christ" (Rom. 8:17)—we're being shaped for that new creation handoff, the whole renewed universe laid at our feet alongside Him (Heb. 2:10; Rev. 21:1–5). We often think of Eternity in terms of a "mansion just over the hilltop," but the reality is galaxies bigger—we're not getting a room; we're getting realms, co-owners with the King in a cosmos scrubbed clean of curse and chaos. This heirship pulls us into the plot, training us through trials to fit the family business.

Performer of the Ages (v. 2c): The next line takes us even deeper into the Son's work: "by whom also he made the worlds" (Heb. 1:2c). Don't picture a divine assembly line churning out planets like widgets off a conveyor belt. The Greek here is *di' hou kai tous aiōnas epoiēsen*—through whom He "performed" or "accomplished" the epochs. That verb *epoiēsen* comes from the root *poiema*, the word for a carefully crafted work of art—think "poem" or "poetry" in English, something shaped with love, skill, and a clear vision in mind. It's not about mass-producing throwaway items; it's the deliberate handiwork of a master artisan, full of beauty, purpose, and those little details that make you step back and say, "Wow, someone poured their heart into this".

To get a feel for how the Greeks used *poiema*, listen to Plato in his dialogue *Timaeus*, where he describes the entire universe as a *poiema* fashioned by the *Demiurge*—a kind of divine craftsman. It's not some sloppy sketch; it's like a master woodworker carving an intricate table from rough oak, every joint fitted just so, every curve sanded smooth to reveal the wood's hidden grain. The *Demiurge* shapes chaos into ordered beauty, step by step, with intention and care. That's the artistry Hebrews evokes here: the Son isn't just the muscle behind creation; He's the creative force, the Poet weaving the grand story of redemption across time itself.

These "worlds" or *aiōnas* aren't just about physical stuff like stars and seas—they're the "ages," the sweeping chapters of history that turn raw existence into a living narrative. From the chaos-to-order burst of Genesis 1, where the Father's "Let us make man in our image" rings out through the Son as co-Creator (Gen. 1:26), to the Angel of the Lord stepping into the burning bush at Sinai, carrying the Father's voice to a stuttering Moses (Exod. 3:2), every moment builds toward Calvary's climax—the *telos*, or goal, where the plot resolves in blood and resurrection (Col. 1:16–17). This takes timeless divine power and threads it through human time like a storyteller unfolding a tale —from Eden's fresh harmony, through Sinai's thunderous covenant, to Golgotha's gut-wrenching grace. It's a divine plot, full of twists that reveal God's character: the Artist who doesn't scrap the flawed canvas but redeems it stroke by stroke.

All revelation rises to this summit. The garden's innocence, the covenant's oath, the law's thunder, the prophet's lament—all their scattered beams converge in one uncreated Light. The Word that once sounded through messengers now steps forth as Man. What came before as echo, now speaks as essence. The Father who once spoke "in sundry times and divers manners" has now spoken finally and fully in His Son (Heb. 1:1–2). Every earlier glimpse was mercy veiled; now mercy has a face. The shadow finds its body, the promise its fulfillment, the yearning its rest.

No longer does man strain through distance and symbol to hear the divine. The Word Himself walks within creation, breathing life into dust once more— stilling seas, cleansing lepers, summoning the dead to rise. The fragments have fallen silent before the fullness. The age of revelation's dawn has given way to its noonday. These are not days of mere waiting for an end, but of standing already within the completed work of God—days illumined by the Son who upholds all things by the word of His power.

Dawning of Glory The poem keeps rolling, painting the Son in strokes that get brighter and more alive with each line. Next up: "Who being the brightness of his glory" (Heb. 1:3a). In Greek, it's *apaugasma tēs doxēs*, which carries this beautiful sense of a beaming radiance, like the first rays of sun spilling over the hill after a long night. It's not a dim bulb or a flickering candle; it's light pouring out, unstoppable and warm, chasing away every shadow in its path. This picks up right where the prophets left off—faint glows of hope in the dark, like Malachi's promise of a coming sun of righteousness with healing in its wings (Mal. 4:2). The Old Testament is full of these glimmering hints: Moses begging for a glimpse of God's glory on Sinai, only to see His back as He passes by because the full shine would overwhelm (Exod. 33:18–23). Or John's Gospel echoing it: "In him was life; and the life was the light of men. And the light shineth in darkness; and the darkness comprehended it not" (John 1:4–5). The word *glory* has the same root as *glow*, like fire on the mountain or cloud filling the temple (Ex. 40:34–35). The prophets gave us the rosy glow, the tease of what's coming—but the Son? He's the dawn itself, the sun cresting full, flooding the whole landscape with color and clarity.

We picture the prophets as that soft light on the horizon just before sunrise—enough to stir hope, but not yet chasing the chill or waking the world. Then Jesus steps in: the bright sun come over the horizon, illuminating everything. It's not subtle; it's transformative. Light isn't just pretty—it's life. Think about your backyard on a crisp fall morning: the sun hits those wilted leaves on the tomato vines, still hanging on after the first frost, and suddenly they stir. Chlorophyll kicks in, pulling energy from the rays to push out one more bit of green, one last tomato maybe. Flowers that drooped overnight perk up, petals unfurling like they're shaking off sleep. That's the Son's glory at work—*apaugasma* quickening what's dead or dying, turning survival mode into full bloom (Isa. 60:1–3: "Arise, shine; for thy light is come, and the glory of the Lord is risen upon thee"). In Him, God's presence isn't hidden behind smoke or stone; it's beaming, inviting us into the warmth, healing what the shadows bruised.

Why do we hide from it? We duck into the shade—our worries, our "I got this" plans, our secret habits—and then wonder why we wither. The light of Christ is our light, the life that should green us up from the inside out, but we court the decay, letting the chill settle in. It's like those leaves choosing the fence corner over the open field: safe from glare, sure, but starved of what makes them thrive. Isaiah saw it coming: nations drawn to that rising glory, but some folks turning away, preferring their dim corners (Isa. 60:2–3). In the garden, Adam and Eve hid from God's walk in the cool (Gen. 3:8); Cain slunk off after his wrong turn (Gen. 4:16); even the prophets faced folks closing their eyes to the glow (Isa. 6:9–10). The Son outshines it all, but the choice stays ours—step into the dawn, or linger in twilight's fade?

This dawning is no abstract theology—it is a summons to awaken. For that first congregation—a mix of the faithful standing firm, the admirers looking on, and the resisters digging in—it was life itself. The prophets' embers had glowed; now the Son's rising brought healing. And the choice remains ours. The dull routine, the hidden hurt, the quiet why bother—all of it waits for His light to break through. This radiance is no static display but a living presence, stirring life in a world gone gray. Why stay in shadow when the Sun stands high? Step into His warmth; let it revive what has withered. The glory shines still—will you reflect it, or cloud it over?

Expression of Essence (v. 3a): The poem becomes even more personal now, as it zooms in on how the Son doesn't just shine—He shows the Father, down to the tiniest detail. "Who being the brightness of his glory, and the express image of his person" (Heb. 1:3a)—we just unpacked that first half, the beaming light of God's presence. But the second part? That's where it hits home: the "express image of his person." In Greek, it's *charaktēr tēs hypostaseōs autou*, words that pack a punch if you slow down and savor them. *Charaktēr* isn't some vague sketch; it's an exact imprint, like the sharp, unerasable stamp you press into soft metal to make a coin. Once it's there, it's forever—every ridge, every line locked in, no smudges or fades. And *hypostasis*? That's the underlying reality, the solid stuff underneath, God's core being, the essence that holds everything together. Put them side by side, and you've got the Son as the perfect, indelible copy of the Father—not a knockoff or a blurry photo, but the real deal etched deep.

You probably have already recognized *charaktēr*: It even slips into our English as "character"—think about that. We say someone's "got character" when their inside matches their outside: words line up with walk, promises hold water, the lines of who they are show clear in what they do. But go deeper: character is who you are inside, the real you that bubbles up when no one's watching. It's what makes you you—

your quirks, your convictions, the stuff that doesn't shift with the wind. That's why we use "character" for letters in the alphabet or those intricate symbols in Chinese writing: those lines and strokes aren't random squiggles; they're fixed, settled marks with a clear, unchangeable meaning. If you know the language, one glance tells you everything—no guesswork, no maybes. Spot an "A" and you know it's the sound that starts "apple" or "anchor." See a Chinese character for "peace," and it unlocks a whole world of calm and wholeness, every stroke locking in the truth.

Now apply that to Jesus: when we look at Him, we know exactly who God is. No fog, no fragments like the old portions. The Son is the express image of the Father, every line of His life etching out the divine reality. Love? See it in the dusty-road welcome for outcasts. Justice? Hear it in the temple-cleansing whip-crack. Mercy? Feel it in the cross's "forgive them" plea. Holiness? Gaze at the sinless walk from manger to empty tomb. Colossians spells it out: He's "the image of the invisible God" (Col. 1:15), the visible stamp of the unseen King. And later in Hebrews, we get the purpose: fix your eyes on Him, the "author and finisher of our faith," who "endured the cross" to re-etch what sin bashed in (Heb. 12:2).

This scene in Matthew comes to mind: the Pharisees, eager to trap Jesus, ask, "Is it lawful to give tribute unto Caesar, or not?" (Matt. 22:17). Jesus asks for a coin, holds it up, and replies, "Whose is this image and superscription?" They answer, "Caesar's." Then comes the thunderclap: "Render therefore unto Caesar the things which are Caesar's; and unto God the things that are God's" (Matt. 22:19–21). On the surface, it sounds like tax advice—pay what's due and move on. But dig deeper, and it's a revelation of ownership. Caesar's image marks his coin; let it return to him. But where is God's image found? On us. "Let us make man in our image, after our likeness" (Gen. 1:26–27). We are living currency of the King— stamped from creation with His likeness and inscription. What, then, do we owe? Everything: our time, our choices, our hearts. Render to God what bears His mark.

Our rebellion in the Garden marred the image we were meant to bear. Eden's bite warped that original stamp—God's likeness—into something cracked and crooked, like a coin struck and bent, its edges nicked and its shine dulled. We began as fresh-minted masterpieces, but sin bent the mold: self over surrender, my will over Thy will. Now we are dented denarii—still marked with the divine inscription, yet scarred from the streets. The Son alone remains unblemished, His *charaktēr* flawless, every line of divinity intact. Through Him we are brought back to the mint—re-stamped, refined, and polished to our pre-rebellion gleam (Rom. 8:29; 2 Cor. 3:18). It is no quick polish, but cross-deep work—yet as certain as the sunrise.

We all carry it—His likeness from day one—but how often do we live as though it were our own to keep? The coin isn't for pocketing; it's for returning to the One who minted it. For the faithful in that first community, this was foundation: you bear God's image, secured forever in the Son—no storm can erase that engraving. For those who acknowledged His divinity yet clung to self-rule, it was a summons to surrender: you've seen the stamp in His healings and His hard sayings—now hand it over and live the life it was struck for. And to the resisters? The lines don't lie; you can't file them off.

Even now, the mirror remains the same. The impatient honk in traffic, the quiet grudge at work, the "just this once" scroll—each leaves a dent in the family likeness. Yet Christ redraws what we mar. His character restores ours, eternal strokes pressed through nails and resurrection.

What if stamped living became our daily practice—not hiding the dents, but letting Him re-mint them? In a world polished by filters and pretense, the image of the Son calls us back to honesty. Render it fresh: a listening ear, a brave boundary, a quiet yes to the hard call. The Master Etcher is faithful—let Him press the lines deeper until His likeness shines through.

Carrier by Mighty Word (v. 3b): The poem's rhythm builds like a gathering storm—steady, unstoppable—as it shifts from the Son's shining image to His sustaining power. "Upholding all things by the word of his power" (Heb. 1:3b)—that's how the King James catches it, but lean in closer, and you hear the motion, the drive behind it all. In Greek, it's *pherōn ta panta tō rhēmati tēs dynameōs autou*: literally, "bearing along all things by the word of His power." *Pherōn* isn't a passive hold; it's active carrying, a forward push—like a strong-backed traveler shouldering a load up a steep path, not just balancing it but moving with it, step by determined step. And that "word of His power"? *Rhēmati tēs dynameōs*—*rhēma* as spoken command, laced with *dynamis*, raw, explosive might. It's not a whisper; it's a decree that does what it says, propelling creation not in circles or stalls, but straight toward purpose.

Imagine everything that exists packed tight in the hold of a massive cargo ship, waves crashing, gales howling, the whole vessel pitching through the storm. *Pherōn* was the word ancients used for that secured freight—crates of spices, bolts of cloth, life's essentials lashed down below decks, safe from the spray and sway. Christ isn't up on deck yelling orders; He's both the captain and the ship itself, the hull and helm, bearing us through every squall. The world is not just chaotically slipping through time with no end and no rudder—no freefall into nothing. His Word is both sail and rudder, the steady thrust keeping us on course. Chaos? Pain? That knot in your gut from the morning headlines? It's all cargo in His hold, harnessed—not happening to Him, but through Him, toward a harbor we can't yet see. As Isaiah foresaw the Servant-Son, He won't "break the bruised reed" or snuff the flickering wick—gentle strength in the gale, carrying the fragile forward till justice flashes like dawn (Isa. 42:1–4).

This isn't some static "upholding," like propping a wobbly table with a folded napkin—mere survival mode, holding the mess in place without fixing it. No, it's dynamic propulsion, a living thrust that turns drift into direction. Colossians echoes it: "In him all things consist" (Col. 1:17)—*synestēken*, holding together not by glue or guesswork, but by the pull of His presence, every atom, every ache woven into the warp. Hebrews doubles down: the same word that sparked "Let there be light" (Gen. 1:3) now bears us along, that *rhēma* as efficacious decree—what He speaks, happens. Creation's fiat? Worlds from void. Gospel's call? "Faith cometh by hearing, and hearing by the word of God" (Rom. 10:17)—dead hearts sparked alive. It's the same voice: "Peace, be still" to Galilee's storm (Mark 4:39), now whispering (and thundering) through our squalls, "This too serves My end."

Our morning scroll through the news or social feeds may tempt us to ask, "Is anyone in control?" The answer is yes—and it is the Son, steady at the helm, rudder in hand, the hold packed full. Your difficult diagnosis, that fractured friendship, the echo of an election—none of these can sink the ship before it reaches its harbor. This is not denial; it is declaration: chaos mastered by the cross, every storm a gust toward glory. For the faithful in that first Hebrew congregation, this truth was ballast against synagogue scorn and Nero's night—your world isn't unraveling; it's rerouting. Admirers felt the tug—a healing touch, a word in season—and were called to step fully aboard, letting His Word drive them beyond partial peace. And to the resisters, the warning remains: the ship is moving; hiding in the hold only delays the dock.

Let Christ do the carrying today. Imagine a small boy on a mighty ship, gripping his pack tightly to keep it safe, when all he has to do is turn it over to the Captain to stow securely. That "what now?" whisper in the quiet? *Rhēma's* reply: forward, held, purposed. This isn't passive maintenance; it's "dynamic propulsion," the power-Word turning inertia to intent. In a world that looks rudderless, claim the cargo-spot: storms serve the Sailor. What's your gale? Let His Word thrust through—news din to dawn song, bruise to bloom. The voyage holds; you're homeward-bound.

Purifier Seated (v. 3c): The poem reaches its emotional peak here, shifting from the Son's radiant image and sustaining power to the heart of the gospel: what He has done for us, and where He sits because of it. "When he had by himself purged our sins, sat down on the right hand of the Majesty on high" (Heb. 1:3c)—this forms a hinge moment, the climax that changes everything. In Greek, *katharismon poiēsamenos* captures the action: "having accomplished purification," with that aorist tense landing like a gavel—decisive, done, no loose ends. This is not a partial wipe-down or a yearly touch-up. It is once-for-all cleansing, the kind that covers every stain from Eden's first bite to your last breath (Heb. 7:27; 9:12, 26).

> **Aorist tense:**
>
> A Greek verb form that presents an action as complete and whole —viewed in a single moment rather than over time. It emphasizes the *fact* of the action, not its duration or repetition.

This changes your view of who you are in Christ. All of our sinfulness is covered. We stand before the Throne in the finished work of Christ. There is nothing we can do, no sin we can commit that can unwork our salvation.

The weight of that "purged"—*katharismon*, from the root for "cleanse"—carries deep temple echoes: blood-sprinkled altars, smoke rising year after year to cover Israel's guilt (Lev. 16:14–16). The old system demanded endless busy-ness—goats and bulls slain on Yom Kippur, sins confessed and carted to the wilderness, but the next year, it all had to be done again (Lev. 16:1–34). No finality existed, no exhale. The high priest hustled from dawn to dusk, hands red, heart heavy, because the job never was never finished. The tabernacle and temple held no chairs because there was no rest—a priesthood that could never sit, for sin kept piling up (Heb. 10:1–4). When the old priest Eli sat, it was not in rest but collapse— his body giving way under the weight of a dying system (1 Sam. 4:18). The seat became a symbol of failure, not fulfillment. Only when Christ offered one perfect sacrifice and sat down at the right hand of God did the work finally rest (Heb. 10:12). Even the Sabbath could not give what the Son secured (Num. 28:9-10, Matt. 12:5); the priests worked while the people paused, but in Him, both rest and righteousness meet.

Jesus changes that completely. He sat down— *ekathisen en dexia*—at the right hand, the place of honor and authority, echoing David's royal psalm: "Sit thou at my right hand, until I make thine enemies thy footstool" (Ps. 110:1). This marks the first time we see a priest enthroned, work consummated, victory sealed. No more standing in the smoke. The Lamb's blood does not just cover—it eradicates, once-for-all (Heb. 9:26). Every sin that you will ever commit is nailed to His cross. Past messes stand forgiven. Future fumbles remain just as covered. You don't have to worry about losing your salvation if you have placed your faith in Christ, your purification is complete. It is not a fragile thread. It is ironclad. High priests paced because their offerings could not stick. Christ's remains eternal, seating Him as King-Priest, our intercessor with the scars to prove it (Heb. 7:25; 1 John 2:1–2).

That seat holds more than comfort. It is not some side chair at the family table. It is "on the right hand of the Majesty on high" (tēs megalōsynēs en hypsēlois), a title towering over emperors and earth-kings, the pinnacle of honor where power meets presence (Acts 2:33; Heb. 8:1). Megalōsynēs evokes the awe-striking "Majesty," like the thunder of Sinai or the glory filling Solomon's temple—transcendent, untouchable (Exod. 15:11; 1 Chron. 29:11). No Roman throne can ever match. Caesar's pomp pales next to this exalted spot, where the Son reigns not as distant dictator but as our brother-king, footstool foes piling up until all is right (Ps. 110:1; Eph. 1:20–22).

For that ancient community—faithful weary from synagogue snubs, admirers tasting but not trusting, resisters clinging to old altars—this brought deep relief. Sins stand purged. The priest sits for them. In our churches today, it offers the same balm. Believers drop the striving and rest in the done. The nagging "what if I blow it?" becomes footstool fodder. His seat remains sure. Admirers glimpse the blood and are invited to immerse in His grace. No half-purges exist. Resisters find the altars empty because the Lamb has bled. They no longer stand alone. They sit with Him.

This accomplished seating extends an invitation to exhale too. In a world of endless to-dos and guilt's grind, believers claim the chair beside His (Eph. 2:6). The work stands wrapped. The Majesty's door stays open. When you recognize how much this purification cost God the Son, we should be avoiding sin as though they were a plague. Avoidance comes not from fear, but from love—clean, seated, free. The next exhale lands in the right hand's rest.

Superior by Exalted Name (v. 4): The poem closes its opening stanza with a final, triumphant flourish, wrapping the Son's portrait in a crown of superiority that sets the stage for the whole book. "Being made so much better than the angels, as he hath by inheritance obtained a more excellent name than they" (Heb. 1:4)—this verse serves as the runway to what follows, launching a direct comparison that carries on through chapters 1 and 2. The Greek translates literally as "having become so much better than the angels," with *kreittōn* emphasizing not just improvement but surpassing excellence in every way. The "how much better" ties straight to the "more excellent name" He has inherited. This name isn't a nickname or honorific add-on; it's the badge of His rank and reality, marking Him as far above angelic messengers.

We linger on this line because it spotlights two different shades of "inheritance" in the poem, each word chosen with care to show the Son's dual hold: one future and full, the other present and unbreakable. Back in verse 2, the first "heir" (*klēronomon*) points to the appointed claim on all creation—the universe as His eventual possession, locked in by the Father's will but not yet fully transferred. As we unpacked it, Christ waits at the right hand "until all things are placed under his feet" (Ps. 110:1; Heb. 10:13), holding back the cosmic handover until His bride (the church) matures to share it in the new heavens and earth. Some inheritances sit dusty in a lawyer's office, untouched and wasting; others demand readiness before claim. Creation falls in that second camp—ours to co-enjoy when the story wraps, but the Son's title deed stands signed since eternity (Rom. 8:17; Heb. 2:10).

Here in verse 4, though, the word shifts to *klēronomēken*—a form that expresses current possession, something already taken hold of, lived in, and owned outright. I translated this "He has inhabited an Exalted Name" because this is the name He lives in now, not one He is waiting to receive. It's not waiting in escrow; He dwells in it now, like stepping into a family estate fully furnished and deed-stamped,

41

no probate delay. Some people inherit land they never visit—it crumbles unseen. Others get keys to a home they can't occupy yet, pacing the driveway in frustration. But this Name? The Son has moved in, claimed every room, and barred the door against eviction. It's His to wield today, the reality that elevates Him above angels—not by birthright alone, but by the cross-earned exaltation (*genomenos* marks that post-resurrection lift, from manger low to throne high; Phil. 2:9; Heb. 2:9).

What is this Name? The poem does not spell it outright, but Scripture makes it plain enough: the core Name is Son—a title that places Him above angels from the start. "Thou art my Son; this day have I begotten thee" (Ps. 2:7). Angels are mighty servants —heralds at Bethlehem, warriors at the tomb—but they are messengers, not heirs (Heb. 1:5–14). The Son's Name speaks of family, intimacy, and authority —the Father's voice echoed in perfect harmony.

Other names in Scripture unfold its fullness: Wonderful Counselor, for wisdom no angel speaks (Isa. 9:6); Mighty God, strength beyond seraphim's reach (Isa. 9:6); Emmanuel, God with us in flesh no heavenly host has worn (Isa. 7:14; Matt. 1:23); and Jesus, the Lord saves, the title only salvation's Captain can bear (Matt. 1:21; Acts 4:12). No archangel is called "Savior." No cherub carries the name "God with us." These are not borrowed titles but the lived reality of divine Sonship—names He has both inherited and inhabits forever.

And beyond them all lies the mystery John glimpsed in Revelation: "a name written, that no man knew, but He Himself" (Rev. 19:12)—a Name so holy that only God can comprehend it. Every title we know is true but partial; that hidden Name remains the eternal depth of who He is, unsearchable and inexhaustible, the secret glory of the Son who reigns above every created order.

For the ancient hearers—faithful ones tempted by angel-lore in synagogue circles, admirers drawn to Jesus' signs but eyeing old safeguards, resisters dismissing Him as mere rabbi—this Name sealed superiority. Angels mediated law (Heb. 2:2), but the Son authors covenant (Heb. 8:6). In our pews, it anchors the same: believers, wear your co-heir Name boldly—Son's possession means yours too, no angelic intermediary needed (Heb. 4:14–16). Admirers, taste the title—it's not distant thunder but daily dwell, inviting you in. Resisters, the Name trumps denial; "Son" echoes from Sinai to empty tomb, demanding allegiance.

This exalted, inhabited Name crowns the poem's rise —better not by degree, but by depth, the relational reality that pulls us from shadows into Son-light. As Boyd observes, it's no "mere title" but the bond that binds creation's plot, exalting the Incarnate One above all. Inherit it with Him: dwell in the Name that names you family, forever.

This unfolds redemption's plot: Father's script, Son's stage—Eden-echo to throne-song, inviting our line.

Application: Heeding the Full Word in Our Last Days

Hebrews' opening poem serves as more than ancient verse. It acts as a steady guide against the pull to drift in these last days—the urgent stretch from the cross to Christ's return, where partial truths tempt but only the Son satisfies completely. In a culture buzzing with "new truths"—apps offering prophecies, visions spreading like wildfire—we pause and refocus. We obey the revelation God has given and embrace the Heir fully. As James Thompson points out, this "final word" in the Son calls for total submission, with neglect leading to greater accountability (Thompson 2008, 22; cf. Heb. 2:2–3). The poem's truths apply directly to the three types of hearers in its original community—and in ours today: the anchored believers who need strengthening, the intrigued admirers who sense the light but hesitate, and the resistant holdouts who prefer shadows. Each group finds a tailored word here, turning head knowledge into heart obedience.

For Anchored Believers: Rest in the Seated Heir's Finished Work

- Grip the peace of purification amid life's stumbles. Tomorrow's failures stand nailed eternally to the cross, freeing you from striving (Heb. 10:14). Grace does not license sin, but covers it completely (Rom. 6:1–2).

- View chaos as cargo secured in His hold. Headlines howl, but the Son's power-word steers every wave toward purpose (Prov. 21:1; Col. 1:17). Your world does not unravel; it advances under His command.

- Live as co-heirs with lavish generosity. You steward the universe now, so test faithfulness in small trusts—like sharing resources or time—as preview of new-creation fullness (2 Cor. 9:8; Rev. 21:7).

- Avoid sin from love's clear logic, not fear's whip. It spreads like plague, harming what God cherishes, so shun it as the poison it is (Ps. 119:11; 1 John 3:6).

- Let trials forge deeper imprint. Allow pressures to conform your character to His, blooming light-life from wilted places (Rom. 8:29; Eph. 5:8).

These truths echo in everyday moments. A grudge against that coworker becomes an obey-the-portion chance—forgive as you stand forgiven (Eph. 4:32). A tight budget tests heir provision—trust through generosity, watching God supply as Heir (Mal. 3:10; Phil. 4:19). As David Guzik observes, this "superior Savior" equips us for the long haul, with Scripture proving His unshakeable grip (Guzik 2015, para. 10). Believers, the poem calls you to seated rest: work done, inheritance unfolding. Let it steady your stride.

For Intrigued Admirers: Step from Sample to Surrender

- You have sampled the light—stickers on your car, prayer in times of trouble, "Amen" on Sunday and other language Monday morning—but control clings like the 5,000 forcing a crown for endless loaves (John 6:15, 66). You may hold Jesus as Messiah in your head, yet not Lord in your heart, and that leaves the spirit hungry (James 2:19).

- Portions prod you forward: obey the glimpse God gives, and dawn breaks fully (John 7:17). A tasted gift invites the whole feast—surrender moves you from shade's edge to sun-soaked center (Ps. 34:8; Heb. 6:4–5).

- Prophets pointed the way; the Son has arrived. No need to linger at signposts when the road leads home.

In our pews, this plays out close to home. That neighbor who says, "Yeah, Jesus died for sins," needs an invitation deeper—share the freedom of seated rest, how it lifts the weight of half-measures. The nagging conviction in your gut stands as portion's call. Pray for a yielding heart, and watch the light quicken what felt dim. Admirers, the poem beckons you across the line: taste no longer suffices. Embrace the Heir; the portions were made for this.

For Resistant Holdouts: Yield to the Dawn's Demand

- Shadows once sufficed—law's familiar rhythm, autonomy's self-made throne—but the Son's dawn exposes the folly of half-dark (Isa. 29:15; John 3:19–20). Prophets issued warnings; now the Son brings judgment and joy in one voice (John 12:48; Heb. 1:2).

- Eden's grab for control repeats in every "no"—yet the Imprint restores what rebellion marred (Gen. 3:5; Col. 3:10). The inherited Name—Emmanuel, Salvation—calls for knees bent in awe (Phil. 2:10–11; Acts 4:12).

- Cultural echoes abound: self-god apps and "my truth" mantras pull back to fragments. The Son's Word, however, carries true—sharp enough to pierce, steady enough to steer (Heb. 4:12; 2 Tim. 3:16).

Church, these last days stretch from cross to crown, with no backups or reruns. Fix your gaze on the Son: see the Father's heart, walk in light-life, carry His purpose forward. Obey the portion at hand. Fullness follows as you yield lingering control to the Heir. Inheritance awaits those who heed.

Prayer

Father,
You have spoken—not in fragments or
whispers, but in the fullness of Your Son.
Forgive us for chasing echoes when the living
Word stands before us.

*Teach our hearts to rest in what He has
already finished, and to live as those who
have heard from Heaven.
Let His light drive out our shadows, His
likeness shape our character,
and His voice steady us when the world
shakes beneath our feet.
When we are tempted to drift, anchor us
again in the One who upholds all things by the
word of His power.
By Your Spirit, help us to treasure the truth
we've received and to practice it with faith
and joy,
until every part of our lives bears the imprint
of Your Son.*

*We ask this in Jesus' name,
Amen.*

2

A Warning Against Drift

On the night of April 14, 1912, the RMS Titanic sliced through the inky waters of the North Atlantic, her hull gleaming under a canopy of stars as she raced toward New York. Launched amid fanfare as the pinnacle of human ingenuity, the ship was a floating palace of innovation: electric lights banished darkness from her corridors, wireless telegraphs connected her to the world beyond the horizon, and sixteen watertight compartments promised invincibility against any sea's fury. Newspapers hailed her as "practically unsinkable," a testament to Edwardian optimism. Aboard, passengers from every walk of life—tycoons in first-class suites, immigrants huddled in steerage—basked in the illusion of safety. The grand staircase spiraled like a cathedral nave, orchestras played ragtime in the lounges, and the air hummed with the thrill of progress. Who could imagine that such a behemoth might bow to a mere berg of ice?

Yet danger whispered long before the collision. Throughout the day, at least six wireless warnings crackled from nearby vessels: ice fields ahead, growlers lurking in the gloom. The messages piled up in the radio room, dismissed as routine by operators more focused on passenger chatter than peril. Captain Edward J. Smith, a veteran of the seas, trusted his vessel's design and the clear night skies. Why slow for shadows? The Titanic pressed on at twenty-two knots, her engines thrumming like a heartbeat, the crew swabbing decks and polishing silver as if the ocean held no threats. Confidence bred complacency; warnings became wallpaper, not wake-up calls.

At 11:40 p.m., a lookout's cry shattered the calm: "Iceberg, right ahead!" Helm hard over, engines reversed—but momentum won. The great ship grazed the berg, a kiss of white against black steel. To those on deck, it seemed a near miss, a shudder and scrape. Below, the truth tore open: five compartments flooded in minutes, the "unsinkable" bulkheads overwhelmed. Panic rippled as lifeboats swung out half-full, the band played on to steady nerves, and the great liner listed into the void. By 2:20 a.m., she slipped beneath the waves, carrying 1,517 souls with her—more than two-thirds of those aboard. The world awoke to headlines of hubris: not a cataclysm of storm or sabotage, but a quiet catastrophe of neglect. Warnings heeded too late, drift unchecked, a harbor of safety passed in the night (Lord 1955, 64–82).

This haunting tale mirrors the quiet peril threading through Hebrews 2, the first of the letter's piercing warnings. Chapter 1 had soared with poetry, unveiling the Son as heir of all, radiance of glory, sustainer of worlds—superior to angels in name and nature. The anonymous author had lifted our eyes to Christ's enthroned majesty. Now comes the drop: "Therefore we ought to give the more earnest heed to the things which we have heard, lest at any time we should let them slip" (v. 1). The "therefore" bridges heaven's heights to earth's hard ground, demanding response from a Supremacy so vast. As William Lane observes, this exhortation functions as the letter's "first parenetic unit," a pastoral pivot from exposition to application, urging vigilance against the subtle slide of indifference (Lane 1991, 38–39).

> ### Paranetic
>
> Greek parainesis — exhortation urging believers to live out revealed truth through obedience, perseverance, and faithfulness.

The phrase "give the more earnest heed" (*prosechōmen*) evokes sailors straining at the helm, eyes fixed on guiding stars amid fog and swell.

Prosechō means to pay close, undivided attention—like a shepherd scanning for wolves or a watchman on the wall. The comparative "more" (*perissoterōs*) intensifies it: if prophets' fragments merited focus, the Son's fullness demands all. The writer of Hebrews is calling on us to grasp onto the truth of Christ as though He were the only safety, because He is. If you were to fall into a raging river, and a log floated by, would you lightly lay your hand on it, or would you wrap your arms around it and grasp on for dear life?

The peril warned against here is not outright revolt, but letting slip (*pararyōmen*)—a nautical term for a ship gliding past harbor mouth, current unnoticed until open sea yawns wide. David deSilva captures the imagery: "The verb suggests a boat carried past its intended destination by a current too subtle to notice until it is too late" (deSilva 2000, 95).

Chances are, if you are reading this book, you are not actively denying the supremacy of Christ or rebelling against the truth of His lordship. We say the right things, affirm the right things, often do the right things. But our thoughts and our wills are directed towards our experience and our faith and hope are in our ingenuity and ability, just like the captain of the Titanic. We may hear the warnings, but we hear it so many times, it just becomes noise. Icebergs happen to other people.

Just as with the Titanic, we don't set out for disaster. We don't plan on rebelling. We just keep going, paying attention to things that don't matter, until the iceberg is against the bow and the harbor is far behind. We say and sing that Jesus is Lord, and live as though I am lord. We love the idea that Jesus loves me, we live in the luxury of the 23rd Psalm without the commitment of the shepherd's rod and staff—resting in green pastures and still waters, but dodging the discipline that keeps us on the path. We nod to the cross's forgiveness on Sunday, then chase our own compass Monday through Saturday, letting the current of comfort and control pull us past the safe inlet of full surrender. The warnings come—through sermons that stir, Scriptures that prick, quiet convictions that whisper—but we assure ourselves, "We're sturdy enough; we'll turn later." And before long, the gospel's great salvation, so freely offered, slips astern like a lighthouse lost in fog. The tragedy isn't in the bold "no," but in the distracted "not yet"—a drift so gentle it feels like sailing, until the cold reality hits and the only anchor left is the one we ignored.

This audience—a Jewish house fellowship—knew the pull. Steeped in temple rhythms and synagogue bonds, they faced Nero's gathering storm (Heb. 10:32–34) and social ostracism. The three types of hearers emerge clear: faithful believers resting in Messiah, yet weary; intrigued admirers assenting to signs but withholding surrender (John 6:66); resistant holdouts clinging to Moses, blind to fulfillment (Heb. 13:9). The writer addresses them all: heed, or harbor lost.

Verse 2 grounds its warning in sharp contrast: "The word spoken by angels was stedfast." The law, delivered through heavenly messengers (Deut. 33:2; Acts 7:38, 53; Gal. 3:19), stood as an unyielding code —firm, binding, and without exception. Every transgression met its due response: stoning for Sabbath violation (Num. 15:32–36), exile for idolatry (2 Kings 17:7–23). Even those partial revelations— spoken through prophets and angels alike—carried weight enough that neglect brought judgment.

Then comes the thunder of verse 3: "How shall we escape, if we neglect so great salvation?" The verb *amelesōmen*—from *ameléō*, "to disregard" or "treat as trivial"—pierces deeper than ignorance. It is not unbelief born of darkness but carelessness in the face of light. This salvation is no small thing; it is monumental. It was **spoken by the Lord**—first sounded from Christ's own lips, from the Sermon on the Mount to the cry, "It is finished." It was **confirmed to us by those who heard Him**—the apostles, eyewitnesses who handled the Word of life (2 Pet. 1:16; 1 John 1:1–3). And it was **attested by God Himself**, who bore witness "with signs and wonders, and with divers miracles, and gifts of the Holy Ghost" (Acts 2:43; 5:12; 1 Cor. 12:4–11).

As the law required, "at the mouth of two or three witnesses shall the matter be established" (Deut. 19:15). Heaven has supplied all three.

The phrase "so great" (*tosautēn*) in verse 3 does not stand alone; it reverberates with the "so much better" (*tosoutō kreittōn*) from chapter 1:4, creating a deliberate echo that measures the Son's superiority not just in rank but in the scale of what He brings. This linguistic link—both using *tosoutos* for "so much"— quantifies salvation's magnitude in ways that pull at the heart, mind, and hope of the reader. It is eschatological, unfolding the end-times reality where the "world to come" (v. 5) breaks in now, not as distant vapor but as inaugurated promise: the day of the Lord that dawned at Calvary (Isa. 2:12; Acts 2:17), where judgment's shadow lifts and the kingdom's light scatters it, culminating in the Appearing of Christ when every knee bows (Heb. 10:37; Phil. 2:10–11). George Guthrie highlights how this "so great" signals the letter's forward pull, transforming abstract doctrine into urgent destiny—salvation not as escape pod but as cosmic renewal, where believers preview the age to come through Spirit-gifts and perseverance.

It is cosmic too, reclaiming the universe-spanning dominion humanity fumbled in Eden. Psalm 8's riddle —"What is man, that thou art mindful of him?" (v. 6)— recalls God's original charter: "Let them have dominion ... over all the earth" (Gen. 1:26, 28). Sin's fracture scattered that rule—thorns choke fields, beasts defy, chaos reigns (Gen. 3:17–19; Rom. 8:20–22). But the Son, "made a little lower than the angels" for suffering's sake (v. 9), restores it all: crowned with glory, He subjects the future world not to angelic overseers but to perfected sons (v. 5, 10). William Lane connects the dots: this salvation "reverses the curse of Genesis 3," harnessing creation's groan under the Heir's footstool (Ps. 110:1; Lane 1991, 45–46). No small fix; it is re-creation's blueprint, where stars realign and seas submit, our co-heir share in the King's full estate (Rom. 8:17; Rev. 21:1–5).

And this salvation is achingly personal—grace shaped to the soul's own wound. It is the tender rescue of wanderers like us, drawn into the Son's willing "taste of death for every man" (v. 9). So great becomes the hush of mercy's reach—not reward for striving, but gift freely poured. The word *geusētai*—to taste—speaks not of a sip but of full sharing; He drank the cup to its dregs, the Captain perfected through pain to lead many sons to glory (v. 10). Through His suffering, our path home was cleared, the way lit by love that went all the way down.

Verse 5 transitions to a horizon of hope: "For unto the angels hath he not put in subjection the world to come, whereof we speak." This "world to come" is no distant dream but an inaugurated reality—the renewed order already breaking in under the

Messiah's reign (Heb. 6:5; 12:26–28). Angels governed the old age, overseeing nations and enforcing the law (Deut. 32:8; Job 1:6). Humanity, however, inherits the new age through the Son's path of suffering and crown (vv. 6–9).

Psalm 8 reframes the human story with wonder: "What is man, that thou art mindful of him? or the son of man, that thou visitest him?" (v. 6). The psalm recalls Adam's original mandate—crowned "a little lower than the angels," set over creation as God's image-bearer and steward (Ps. 8:4–6; Gen. 1:26–28). The very name *Adam* means one with blood—a being of dust infused with life, earthly yet bearing heaven's imprint. He stood as the First Man, the head of humanity under God's good rule, charged to fill the earth and exercise dominion in harmony with his Maker. Yet his deliberate rebellion shattered that calling. In choosing self-rule over God's word, Adam ushered in sin's curse, fracturing the divine image and scattering human authority into chaos—thorns in the ground, strife among brothers, death's shadow over all (Gen. 3:1–19; Rom. 5:12).

The Son arrives as the Second Adam—the obedient Head who restores what the first lost (1 Cor. 15:45–47; Rom. 5:12–19). "Made a little lower than the angels" in incarnation, He entered the same flesh and blood (Adam) to bear sin's full weight, and rose crowned with glory and honor through the suffering of death (v. 9). His "taste of death for every man" stands as deliberate substitution—grace drinking the cup rebellion filled. By the mercy of God, He drains it dry, turning curse to conquest and bondage to brotherhood. Through suffering, the Captain of salvation is perfected, completing His work to bring many sons to glory (v. 10).

Where Adam's choice brought death to all, the Second Adam's obedience brings life—reclaiming dominion not through might alone, but through humble solidarity with us, His brothers and sisters. As Paul writes, "For as by one man's disobedience many were made sinners, so by the obedience of one shall many be made righteous" (Rom. 5:19). This cosmic reclamation feels deeply personal: the Son's low road mirrors our broken paths; His crown, our future glory —calling us from rebellion's wreckage to restored rule under the true Head. This is the heart of "so great salvation"—not mere pardon, but paradise previewed, where humanity's high call glows anew in the light of the One who came lower to lift us higher.

Verse 10 turns from warning to wonder: "For it became him, for whom are all things, and by whom are all things, in bringing many sons unto glory, to make the captain of their salvation perfect through sufferings." The phrase it became him (*eprēpen autō*) means "it was fitting." In other words, the path God chose was not accidental or unfortunate; it was morally beautiful—the one story that best displays His wisdom, justice, mercy, and love. The One "for whom" and "by whom" all things exist determined that the way to bring "many sons unto glory" ran straight through the furnace of the Son's suffering.

The "Captain" (*archēgos*) is the pioneer—the first over the wall, the founder who charts the course for all who follow. Christ does not call from the shore; He enters the waters Himself, swimming the channel before turning to reach for us. His perfection (*teleioō*) does not suggest moral lack but mission completed. The Captain is perfected in the sense that He finishes the course He came to run—the rescue accomplished through suffering, not apart from it.

The work was not perfected in Bethlehem's manger or Nazareth's workshops, but at Golgotha. The cradle introduced His humanity; the cross unveiled His divinity in its fullest light. If chapter 1 enthrones the Son above the angels, chapter 2 enthrones the cross as His coronation. The manger showed His humility; the cross displayed His majesty.

Glory, then, is not the sparkle that follows pain—it is the fire that burns within it (John 17). When Jesus prayed, "Father, glorify Thy Son," He was not asking to escape the nails, but to fulfill their purpose. He looked through the suffering to the splendor woven inside it. The wood of the cross was the wood of His throne; the wounds were the royal seal of a Kingdom won through love.

We tend to think of glory as applause, as radiance untouched by grime, but heaven's definition is different. Glory is what happens when holiness collides with suffering and nothing breaks but the chains. The gold of divine character only gleams when pressed by fire. At Calvary, suffering did not tarnish the Son's perfection—it polished it to brilliance. The universe had seen God's power in creation, His justice in the law, His providence in Israel's history, but only at the cross did it see His heart unveiled: mercy glowing through agony, strength revealed in surrender.

The cross is not a detour on the way to glory; it is the way. Christ was not crowned after He bled but by His bleeding. His wounds are the jewels of His kingship. The soldiers thought they were shaming Him with thorns, but they were unknowingly weaving His diadem. Every hammer blow echoed heaven's "Amen." Every lash became an inscription of love across eternity's scroll.

And so the pattern holds: if the Captain's glory was shaped in suffering, the crew's will be too. We burn to shine. We are refined to reflect. The crown that waits for us is cut from the same wood that bore Him. Our trials do not compete with His glory—they complete it in us (Rom. 8:17; 2 Cor. 4:17). The Christian's suffering is not wasted pain but borrowed light; every tear is a prism catching some facet of His radiance. To follow Christ is to walk not away from the fire but through it, discovering that the very heat that scorches the world makes the saints sparkle.

If the cross is the Captain's coronation, then His glory is not solitary light but shared flame. Verse 11 continues, "For both he that sanctifieth and they who are sanctified are all of one: for which cause he is not ashamed to call them brethren." What a wonder! The One who holds galaxies together is not ashamed to clasp hands with the dust He shaped. The fire that refines the Captain now runs through His people. The same suffering that perfected Him is the forge in which He perfects us. When God calls His sons to glory, He calls them into the same furnace where His Son stood radiant amid the coals.

"He that sanctifieth"—Christ Himself—is the One who makes holy, who burns away what cannot last. "They who are sanctified"—that's us—stand in the glow of His purifying work. And the phrase "are all of one" means of one stock, one source, one family. The divine and the human now share a single bloodline— the blood of the covenant, poured at Calvary. Think of it: the holy and the sinful joined, not by merit, but by mercy's DNA.

And so He is not ashamed to call them brethren. He doesn't whisper our names behind closed doors or blush when our failures are mentioned. He stands in the midst of the assembly and sings (v. 12): "I will declare thy name unto my brethren, in the midst of the church will I sing praise unto thee." That is the risen Christ, leading the hymn, lifting the same voice that once cried "It is finished," now saying, "Father, they're Mine."

Our world ties honor to ease and status, but heaven ties it to solidarity. The Captain of our salvation is not aloof, watching from the bridge while the crew scrambles below deck. He stepped down into the bilge water, took the bucket, and bailed with us. He is "the sanctifier" who has walked every deck plank of human suffering—tempted, weary, misunderstood, betrayed—and yet without sin. His glory is not the absence of wounds but the presence of love that kept shining through them.

So when we suffer, we do not lose glory—we find it. We suffer with Christ, and He suffers in us. Every hardship faithfully borne becomes a note in the hymn He is still singing. Every trial endured becomes another spark in the shared flame that ties heaven to earth. He is not ashamed to call us brethren because, through the cross, we share His likeness. Glory does not wait until the pain ends; it starts where surrender begins. The Captain glows, and we, His crew, glow with Him.

Pastorally, that matters. Shame whispers, "You don't belong. Real saints don't struggle like you." Scripture answers: He is not ashamed to call you brother/sister. If the Captain is unashamed, why should you be? Drift often begins with shame's small turn of the rudder—avoiding prayer, skipping fellowship, silencing confession. The antidote is not gritted teeth; it is His voice in the congregation: "Mine."

If the glory of Christ is shared in suffering, it is also shared in victory. Verse 14 opens the triumph:

> "Forasmuch then as the children are partakers of flesh and blood, he also himself likewise took part of the same; that through death he might destroy him that had the power of death, that is, the devil; and deliver them who through fear of death were all their lifetime subject to bondage."

The Captain did not wage this war from the bridge; He came down into the waterlogged hold. He took on our flesh and blood, not in appearance only, but in reality —frail skin, tired muscles, the full weight of human vulnerability. The phrase "took part" (*meteschēn*) means He shared fully. He didn't sample humanity— He swallowed it whole. The Infinite stepped into finitude; the Immortal put on mortality. Why? So that He could storm death from the inside out.

"Through death He might destroy him that had the power of death." Destroy—*katargēsē*—means to render powerless, to make void. He didn't annihilate the devil's existence; He shattered the devil's dominion. Death was Satan's trump card, the terror by which he held mankind hostage. But when Jesus died, the power source of that terror was unplugged. The grave swallowed Him—and choked. Death digested Deity and could not hold Him. The Captain went down into the depths, found the lock, and broke it from within. Now the keys jingle on His belt (Rev. 1:18).

Death remains, but it's been declawed. The Christian still dies, but never alone. Death has become the servant of resurrection, the midnight before dawn. Once, we feared it as the captain of another ship— cold, dark, inevitable. Now we see it as a rowboat Christ Himself will use to ferry us home. Through His dying, He "delivers them who through fear of death were all their lifetime subject to bondage."

The fear of death is not just dread of dying; it is the subtle tyranny of self-preservation. It's what keeps us cautious when God calls us to courage, comfortable when He calls us to costly love. It builds invisible fences around our obedience. That fear whispers, "Don't risk too much—don't forgive too far—don't burn too bright." But Christ burned, and in burning, broke the fear forever. He calls us not to survive, but to shine. The death of death is the dawn of fearless faith.

When Paul said, "I will rather glory in my infirmities, that the power of Christ may rest upon me," (2 Cor. 12:9), he was echoing this very truth. He had found that strength hides in surrender, power in weakness, and glory in pain. Death was no longer master; it had become a mirror, showing the life of Christ reflected in the cracked glass of our mortality.

We live now as those who cannot lose. The worst that can happen already happened—to Christ—and He walked out the other side holding victory like a torch. He tasted every drop of death's bitterness so that when our lips touch it, it will be sweet with grace. "O death, where is thy sting? O grave, where is thy victory?" (1 Cor. 15:55). The sting has been drawn, the venom spent. We fear no longer the deep, because the Captain has crossed it first.

If Christ's victory over death frees us from fear, His priesthood secures us in fellowship. Verse 16 turns the thought again:

> *"For verily he took not on him the nature of angels; but he took on him the seed of Abraham."*

The writer repeats the contrast—angels versus humanity—to fix our focus on the wonder of the incarnation. Christ did not come to redeem the celestial order; He stooped lower still, entering Abraham's line, the dust-path of promise. He passed by the shining seraphs to share the burden of sinners. This is not the rescue of distant pity, but of familial mercy. The Savior did not merely visit the human condition; He became one of us.

Verse 17 drives it deeper:

> "Wherefore in all things it behoved him to be made like unto his brethren, that he might be a merciful and faithful high priest in things pertaining to God, to make reconciliation for the sins of the people."

"Behoved" (*opheilen*) means He was obligated—not by compulsion, but by covenant love. Divine justice demanded it, and divine mercy desired it. He was made "like unto His brethren" not in part but in all things—hunger, fatigue, grief, rejection, temptation, even the long silence of unanswered prayers. The Son who created all entered the ache of all. He is merciful toward us because He has walked in our weakness, and faithful toward the Father because He fulfilled every command. In Him, mercy and faithfulness finally meet, righteousness and peace kiss (Ps. 85:10).

And what was the purpose? "To make reconciliation for the sins of the people." The word *hilaskesthai* means to propitiate—to satisfy justice, to bridge the breach. Here stands the mystery at the heart of Hebrews: God's wrath met God's love in God's Son, and both were satisfied. Atonement was not a negotiation between offended deity and pleading humanity; it was God Himself providing the sacrifice. The High Priest carried no lamb up Calvary's hill—He was the Lamb.

Then verse 18 closes the circle:

"For in that he himself hath suffered being tempted, he is able to succor them that are tempted."

The Captain who bled now stands at the helm, hand still scarred, ready to steady those whose faith wavers in the storm. The word "succor" (*boēthēsai*) means to run to the cry. He does not wait for polished prayers or formal petitions; He runs. The Savior who once climbed the hill of suffering now climbs into our trials with us. The One who conquered death does not leave His soldiers limping alone on the field—He comes at the sound of their distress call.

This is the heartbeat of "so great salvation." We do not serve a distant deity unmoved by our pain; we follow a Captain who has walked every valley, shouldered every sorrow, and still shines through the smoke. He is not ashamed to call us brothers, not unwilling to enter our need, not too holy to touch our hurt. He is merciful—feeling our weakness; faithful—never failing His word; able—strong enough to save to the uttermost.

The unshakable kingdom begins here: not on a throne of gold, but on a cross of wood. The crown gleamed first with blood before it ever gleamed with glory. Our salvation was perfected not in escape from suffering, but in the God who entered it, conquered it, and turned it into the pathway home.

Summary

Hebrews 2 presses the church to vigilance—to heed what has been heard, lest the harbor of salvation slip behind unnoticed. The warning is not hurled at rebels, but whispered to the distracted. We do not fall from faith by force; we drift from it by neglect. The chapter opens with the peril of inattention and ends with the power of incarnation. In between stands the unshakable Captain—Christ our Pioneer—who entered suffering not as accident but appointment.

Through His incarnation, the Son stepped below angels; through His crucifixion, He rose above them. The "so great salvation" is not merely escape from wrath but entrance into dominion—the restoration of humanity's lost glory through the obedience of a suffering Savior. Bethlehem revealed His nearness; Calvary revealed His nature. The cross was no humiliation but His coronation. His wounds are not blemishes but badges of perfection. The glory of God shines most clearly through the cracks of pain, where holiness meets humanity and love outlasts agony.

In Christ, suffering became the forge of completion. Through death, He destroyed the one who wielded death's power, and in doing so broke fear's grip on all who follow Him. As both High Priest and Brother, He brings many sons to glory—not by removing their pain but by redeeming it. The Son of God became Son of Man, so that sons of men might become sons of God. The kingdom He builds cannot be shaken because its cornerstone was laid in suffering and sealed in blood.

Application

The warning against drift reaches into every pew, every pulpit, every heart that coasts. It is easy to let go, not by open rebellion but by quiet inattention. Faith does not collapse in a storm; it erodes in the calm. We lose our fire not when the sea rages, but when it seems still and safe. The Titanic didn't sink because of defiance, but because of distraction. The same slow drift threatens our souls when we admire Christ but do not anchor in Him.

Look again at the Captain. His course did not avoid pain—it went straight through it. If the Captain's crown was hammered from suffering, why do we expect ours to be woven from comfort? To share His glory is to share His path: through fire, into flame. The Christian does not glow despite affliction, but through it. As we follow the One who was made perfect through suffering, every trial becomes a chance for glory to break out from within us.

Hebrews calls us not merely to listen to truth but to cling to it—to wrap both arms around the gospel as though it were the only thing keeping us from the current. Because it is. Don't drift past the harbor. Don't polish the decks of your own ship while the Captain calls you aboard His. Give more earnest heed. Hold fast to what you have heard, lest it slip. For the hands that hold you still bear the marks of His love.

Prayer

Father,
We thank You that our salvation is not fragile,
because our Savior is not. Teach us to see
Your glory not only in triumph but in trial, To
trust the wounds that saved us,
To walk the path our Captain walked—
Not fearing the fire, but glowing within it.
Keep us from drift.
Anchor our hearts in Christ,
That we might burn and not be consumed,
Shine and not grow dim,
Suffer and still sing.
For You have called us sons,
And You are not ashamed to call us Yours.
In Jesus' name, Amen.

3

Labor to Rest: The Apostle and High Priest of Our Confession

The writer of Hebrews continues to press the same great theme: Christ is superior. He has already shown Him superior in revelation (chapter 1) and in incarnation (chapter 2). Now the argument advances—Christ is the superior Apostle and the superior Builder of God's house.

"Wherefore, holy brethren, partakers of the heavenly calling, consider the Apostle and High Priest of our profession, Christ Jesus" (Heb. 3:1).

When we hear the word *apostle*, our minds rush to the Twelve. They were hand-picked envoys of the incarnate Christ, eyewitnesses of His resurrection, carriers of His authority. Judas fell; Paul replaced him;

and those twelve names now gleam upon the foundation stones of the New Jerusalem (Rev. 21:14). Their witness was unique—an unrepeatable office anchored in firsthand revelation. Yet the word itself, *apostolos*, means simply one who is sent. Its power lies not in the title but in the sending.

The Twelve were apostles of Christ—commissioned directly by the risen Lord, invested with signs and wonders to authenticate their message, tasked with writing and propagating the New Testament. But the New Testament also uses the term more broadly for apostles of the church: trusted messengers like Epaphroditus, who carried the church's compassion and gifts to Paul in prison (Phil. 2:25), or Barnabas and Silas, sent to strengthen young congregations (Acts 13:2–3; 15:22). These were not founders of new revelation but faithful couriers of the one already delivered. They bore the heart of the church where the church itself could not go.

In that sense, every generation of missionaries still walks in apostolic footsteps—not in the authority of the Twelve, but in their obedience. The pattern endures: a sending body, a called servant, a world in need of Christ's Word. The true mark of an apostle is not office but obedience—feet willing to go, lips ready to speak, hearts anchored in the One who first said, "As my Father hath sent me, even so send I you" (John 20:21).

But Hebrews takes the idea further still, lifting our eyes beyond the apostles of the church to what might be called the apostles of God the Father. The writer sets two side by side: Moses and Christ. Both were sent ones—both carried heaven's commission into human history—but the contrast between them unveils the very heart of the gospel.

Moses stands as the first great apostle of the Old Covenant. God called to him from the burning bush— flame without fuel, presence without consumption— and said, "Come now therefore, and I will send thee unto Pharaoh" (Exod. 3:10). Moses was sent: to confront tyranny, to redeem slaves, to deliver the Word of God sealed in covenant and stone. His life was a mission from start to finish—drawn from the Nile, drawn into the desert, drawn up the mountain to hear the voice that shakes earth and heaven. He was faithful as a servant in all God's house, bearing testimony to what was yet to come (Heb. 3:5).

And yet, even Moses knew his commission was incomplete. As his days neared their close, the Lord told him something astonishing: "I will raise them up a Prophet from among their brethren, like unto thee, and will put my words in his mouth; and he shall speak unto them all that I shall command him" (Deut. 18:18). That was a promise—a prophetic whisper across the ages—that another apostle would come, one who would speak not merely about God, but as

God. Moses was sent from the bush; Christ was sent from the bosom of the Father (John 1:18).

Where Moses led the people out of bondage, Jesus leads them out of sin. Where Moses brought the law written on stone, Jesus writes grace upon the heart. Where Moses entered the tent to intercede for a guilty nation, Jesus entered the heavens to intercede for a redeemed one. Moses' mission was a shadow; Christ's was the substance. The first apostle pointed to deliverance; the final Apostle became that deliverance.

The writer of Hebrews presses the image further. Having set Moses and Christ side by side, he invites us to look upward—past the servant to the Son, past the stones of duty to the Builder Himself. "For this man was counted worthy of more glory than Moses, inasmuch as he who hath builded the house hath more honour than the house" (Heb. 3:3).

The "house" here is not a temple of cedar or stone, but the household of faith—the community God is constructing through the ages. Every redeemed soul becomes a living beam, every act of trust another pillar in the dwelling of the Most High. Moses served faithfully within that structure, carrying materials of revelation and law, but Christ designed the blueprint. Moses could polish the silver; Christ forged the gold. The servant tends the house—the Son owns it.

And the builder's claim reaches back to creation itself. "He that built all things is God" (v. 4). The carpenter of Nazareth was no mere craftsman of wood and nails; the galaxies were His handiwork long before Golgotha's beams. When the eternal Word became flesh, the Architect stepped onto His own construction site. The same hands that shaped the Milky Way now stretched out in mercy to shape new hearts.

This is the turning point: Moses was faithful in God's house; Christ is faithful over it. Moses maintained what was entrusted; Christ sustains what He Himself designed. The apostle of Sinai could carry instructions; the apostle of Calvary carries inheritance. Under Moses, the people were tenants under command; under Christ, they become children at home.

The law Moses brought down from the mountain was holy, but it could not heal. It thundered commands but gave no strength to obey them. It was light without warmth, truth without power. The tablets came from the hand of God, but the heart of man remained stone. The law's purpose was never to save—it was to reveal our need for saving. As Paul would elsewhere write, "The law was our schoolmaster to bring us unto Christ" (Gal. 3:24).

Yet Israel mistook the school for the Savior. They saw in Moses not a servant pointing forward, but a standard to surpass. When they heard the words,

79

"This do, and thou shalt live," they thought life came through doing. But life has always come through believing. They thought the covenant of Sinai was a ladder to climb; it was a mirror to humble. They believed their keeping of the law could earn rest; instead, their striving only deepened their unrest.

Moses led them out of Egypt, through the Red Sea, into the wilderness where God revealed His power and His law. Every morning manna testified that God could be trusted. Every evening the pillar of fire testified that God was near. But when they stood at the border of Canaan—the land of promise, the place of rest—they turned back in unbelief. They had seen the sea divide and bread fall from heaven, yet their hearts hardened.

"Wherefore," the Lord said, "I was grieved with that generation... So I sware in my wrath, They shall not enter into my rest" (Heb. 3:10–11). They wandered until their bones whitened the desert. The same feet that stepped through parted waters never stepped across the Jordan. What they lacked was not obedience alone—it was faith that obeys.

The lesson endures. Law without faith still leads to exhaustion. Many today wander the same wilderness —striving to earn favor, to prove worth, to clean what only grace can cleanse. Like Israel, they carry the tablets but miss the temple. They measure holiness by performance and find no rest for their souls.

But God's promise remains open. "There remaineth therefore a rest to the people of God" (Heb. 4:9). The rest Moses could not give, Jesus has secured. On the cross He cried, "It is finished," and heaven echoed the seventh day: "God did rest from all His works" (4:4). When Christ died, the work was complete. When He rose, the door to rest swung open. The toil of law was ended; the labor of faith began.

To rest in Christ is not laziness—it is trust. It is ceasing from self-righteous labor and leaning wholly on the righteousness of Another. "He also hath ceased from his own works, as God did from his" (4:10). Rest does not mean doing nothing; it means nothing left to earn.

When Scripture says, "God did rest the seventh day from all His works" (Heb. 4:4), it does not mean the Almighty collapsed from exertion. The Creator does not grow weary, nor does omnipotence run out of breath. The Sabbath was never about recovery; it was about completion. God rested because there was nothing left to do. Every atom stood in its appointed place, every law of physics set to song, every creature alive in the joy of its Maker's word. When He looked upon creation and said, "It is very good," He wasn't marking the end of a struggle—He was celebrating a finished masterpiece.

Divine rest is not the pause of fatigue but the posture of fulfillment. It is the satisfaction of perfect work, the quiet delight of a job wholly done. The first Sabbath was the world's first doxology—a cosmic "Amen." It was God rejoicing in what He Himself had accomplished. The rest of Genesis 2 was not the absence of activity but the presence of harmony—everything moving as it should, nothing striving against its design.

And that same rest—Eden's calm, creation's wholeness—is what Christ came to restore. When He bowed His head upon the cross and declared, "It is finished," heaven heard an echo of Genesis 2. Another Sabbath dawned, not at the end of creation but at the end of redemption. The Father rested from forming worlds; the Son rested from saving souls.

For the believer, to enter God's rest is to enter that divine satisfaction—to live in the joy of something already accomplished. It is to cease from our anxious attempts to improve what Christ has perfected. The work is done. The masterpiece is finished. The brush has been set down.

Rest, then, is not retreat from labor but rejoicing in completion. It is worship through trust—sabbath of the soul. To believe in Christ is to say, "There is nothing left for me to add, nothing left for me to fix. My salvation is complete because His work is complete." The same God who looked at creation and said, "It is very good," now looks at every believer hidden in Christ and says the same.

But unbelief always turns rest into wandering. The Israelites stood on the edge of promise, their tents within sight of vineyards they would never taste, and yet they turned back. They had seen the Red Sea split, the manna fall, the rock give water, and still they doubted that the God who began their deliverance could finish it. That is the tragedy of unbelief—it refuses to rest in what God has already done. It insists on carrying burdens Christ has already borne.

Unbelief keeps the soul pacing the desert long after the door to Canaan stands open. It prays but never trusts, works but never worships, moves but never arrives. It sings about freedom while secretly clutching the chains of self-effort. Like Israel, it builds tabernacles to anxiety and altars to performance, hoping that somewhere in the exhaustion God will finally be pleased.

But God does not meet us in the wilderness of striving; He calls us into the land of rest. Faith crosses over where fear hesitates. Faith looks at the finished work and says, "It is enough." Faith stops wandering because it believes the work is done.

Unbelief will die measuring its progress; faith will live rejoicing in completion. The author's warning is sharp: "Take heed, brethren, lest there be in any of you an evil heart of unbelief, in departing from the living God" (3:12). Faith is not an opinion; it is obedience that trusts. The invitation still rings: "Today if ye will hear his voice, harden not your hearts."

Hebrews 4 turns the warning into a promise. The rest Israel missed remains open to all who believe. "There remaineth therefore a rest to the people of God" (4:9). God's own rest on the seventh day wasn't weariness but completion. He rested because the work was done. Likewise, Christ's cross finished the work of redemption. To rest in Him is to cease from our own labors—our striving for merit—and to trust the finished work of God.

Then comes the paradox: "Let us labour therefore to enter into that rest." Rest takes effort. It means fighting pride, resisting self-reliance, and holding fast our confidence firm to the end. The battle of the believer is to keep resting in grace.

The writer closes this portion with a weapon forged in heaven's fire:

"For the word of God is quick, and powerful, and sharper than any two-edged sword, piercing even to the dividing asunder of soul and spirit, and of the joints and marrow, and is a discerner of the thoughts and intents of the heart."

The same Word that once spoke galaxies into being now searches the human heart. It is living—not a dead letter, not a record of what God once said, but the present voice of the living God. It does not sleep in ink; it breathes. Every time we open the Scriptures, the Author is in the room.

The Word is powerful—energetic, active, uncontainable. It can break what nothing else can bend, mend what nothing else can heal, and ignite what nothing else can kindle. It is no passive text; it is divine surgery. The Spirit wields it with precision, cutting away deceit, exposing unbelief, and dividing the superficial from the spiritual.

It pierces "to the dividing asunder of soul and spirit." The soul is where our emotions and impulses dwell; the spirit is where faith and communion with God live. Often we confuse the two. We mistake enthusiasm for devotion, or sentiment for surrender. But the Word cuts through the confusion. It discerns what springs from self and what springs from the Spirit.

It also reaches "to the joints and marrow"—that is, to the hidden places, the connective tissue of our intentions. Nothing is off limits. The Word knows where our motives hide, where our pride disguises itself as service, where our fear dresses up as prudence. Before its edge, every mask falls away.

And then comes the verdict: "Neither is there any creature that is not manifest in His sight: but all things are naked and opened unto the eyes of Him with whom we have to do" (4:13). God's Word and God's gaze are one. The same voice that spoke the universe into order now speaks through the page to bring our hearts into alignment. The Word doesn't simply reveal sin—it reveals self. It uncovers whether our rest is genuine or merely rehearsed.

When the sword pierces, it is not to destroy but to heal. The divine incision cuts away everything that keeps us from rest. The same hand that holds the blade also binds the wound. When we submit to the Word, we discover that rest is not the absence of examination but the fruit of surrender. The heart cannot truly rest until it is wholly open before God.

Summary

The argument of Hebrews 3–4 unfolds like a two-act drama:

- Act I: Moses the servant builds under orders; Christ the Son builds as Lord. The faithfulness of Moses points to the greater faithfulness of Christ.

- Act II: Israel's unbelief becomes the warning; the promise of rest becomes the invitation. Rest is not idleness—it is trust. To believe is to stop building our own tower and to dwell in the house already finished by the Son.

The Word of God keeps this rest alive within us. It divides soul and spirit, revealing whether our obedience flows from faith or fear. Thus the believer's labor is not moral performance but spiritual vigilance —to keep believing, to keep resting, to keep looking to Jesus, the Apostle and High Priest of our confession.

Application

1. **Cease from Self-Righteous Labor.** The gospel calls us to stop trying to impress God. Every "good work" done to earn His favor is a declaration that Christ's cross was insufficient. Lay it down. Rest in His finished work.

2. **Trust When Sight Fails.** Israel faltered at the edge of Canaan because the giants looked bigger than God's promise. Faith steps forward anyway. Your "Canaan" may be forgiveness, reconciliation, or surrender—but the same principle stands: believe and enter.

3. **Labor to Stay Resting.** Rest requires discipline. Pride, comparison, and performance creep in daily. You must labor to keep your soul quiet in His sufficiency—through Word, prayer, and fellowship.

4. **Let the Word Examine You.** The living Word exposes motives. It will interrupt your temper before you explode, your vanity before you boast, your despair before you quit. Keep the sword unsheathed. Meditate on it, murmur it to yourself through the day, and let it reshape you from within.

Prayer

Father,
We thank You for the finished work of Your
Son. Forgive us for every attempt to earn
what grace has already given. Teach us to rest
—to cease from our labors and trust in Christ
alone. Pierce us with Your living Word until
every false motive falls away, and let our
hearts stay soft to hear Your voice "today."
Grant us the diligence that leads to rest, the
humility that welcomes grace, and the faith
that endures to the end.
In Jesus' name we pray. Amen.

4

Christ Our High Priest

The argument of Hebrews moves now from Christ's superiority over angels and apostles to His superiority as High Priest. This title appears nowhere else in the New Testament; the writer of Hebrews alone unfolds its glory. Here the church beholds her Lord not merely as the Messenger of the covenant but as the Mediator of it—One who represents man to God and God to man.

> *Seeing then that we have a great high priest, that is passed into the heavens, Jesus the Son of God, let us hold fast our profession.*

> *For we have not an high priest which cannot be touched with the feeling of our infirmities; but was in all points tempted like as we are, yet without sin.*

Let us therefore come boldly unto the throne of grace, that we may obtain mercy, and find grace to help in time of need. (Hebrews 4:14-16)

The Humanity and Sympathy of Christ (Hebrews 4:14 – 5:3)

Seeing then that we have a great high priest, that is passed into the heavens, Jesus the Son of God, let us hold fast our profession (Heb. 4:14).

The high priest of Israel stood but once a year within the veil on the Day of Atonement (Lev. 16). Bearing the blood of a sacrifice first for himself and then for the people, he entered a chamber veiled from sight, a copy and shadow of heavenly things. His ministry confessed its own insufficiency: he must return again the next year, and the next—because his sin and the people's sin were unending, and because the blood he carried could never purge the conscience, only sanctify to the purifying of the flesh. He ministered standing, for his work was never finished.

But Christ, our great High Priest, having offered Himself—not the blood of another, but His own—once for all, passed into the heavens (Heb. 9:12; 4:14). He did not enter a tent made with hands, that is to say, not of this building, but the true sanctuary, the immediate presence of God. There, by one offering, He obtained eternal redemption, not an annual reprieve. The rent veil declares the way opened; the empty tomb declares death defeated; and His session —His taking of the seat—declares the sacrifice accepted. Earth's priests stood daily because their service could not conclude; the Son sat down on the right hand of the Majesty on high (Heb. 1:3; 10:12), because nothing remains to be added. His ascension is His enthronement, and His enthronement is the visible proof that redemption is accomplished and the covenant secured forever.

Unlike the sons of Aaron, this Priest is both sympathetic and sinless:

> *For we have not an high priest which cannot be touched with the feeling of our infirmities; but was in all points tempted like as we are, yet without sin (4:15).*

Temptation's pressure did not lessen in Him because of sinlessness—it deepened. Every temptation that touches fallen man touched Him, yet without the inward traitor that makes our resistance brief. The unyielding heart feels the full weight of trial. The sinner collapses under temptation's early gusts; Christ endured the storm entire. Where we yield and find release, He stood and bore its full fury. The longer one resists, the heavier the pull becomes; therefore His resistance was not lighter, but infinitely heavier, for He never yielded. He drank temptation's cup to the dregs and remained pure. He knows what it is to hunger, to thirst, to be lonely, to be misunderstood, to stand in the presence of the Tempter himself—and yet He never sinned. He who never fell knows the battle better than any who have. Therefore He is touched—He feels the throbbing of our frailty, the ache of our humanity—yet remains undefiled, a High Priest both compassionate and victorious, who can meet every trembling soul at the throne of grace and say, "I know."

Every high priest taken from among men is "ordained for men in things pertaining to God" (5:1). He stands as a bridge between the guilty and the Holy, offering gifts and sacrifices for sins—not his own devising, but according to divine appointment. Yet that very appointment reveals the weakness of the office. The priest ministers as one who shares the need he represents. He can be gentle toward the ignorant and wayward because he, too, is compassed with infirmity. His sympathy is real, but it is sympathy of the fallen with the fallen. He knows the pang of guilt because guilt beats in his own breast. He stands at the altar as both advocate and offender. Before he can plead for Israel, he must cleanse himself; before he can offer for others, he must offer for his own sin. His hands that sprinkle the blood are stained by the very corruption it is meant to cover. His service was necessary—it preserved a shadow of access, it declared that sin demanded atonement—but it was never sufficient. The smoke rose upward, but the conscience remained unpurged; the veil still hung between man and God.

Yet being human himself, he ministers with a mixture of compassion and corruption. His sympathy is genuine, but it is sympathy of the fallen with the fallen. His own frailty gives him feeling, yet it also clouds his sight. He may discern pain, but not always perceive prayer. Eli was such a priest. When Hannah stood before the tabernacle at Shiloh, in bitterness of soul, and prayed unto the Lord, and wept sore (1 Samuel 1:10), Eli "marked her mouth and thought her drunken" (1 Samuel 1:12–14). He could see her anguish but could not hear her heart. So limited is the priest who bears the same infirmity he is called to heal. Before he can atone for others, he must first atone for himself. His hands tremble with guilt even as he offers blood for guilt. His service was necessary, but never sufficient—its compassion marred by corruption, its ministry clouded by misunderstanding.

Christ fulfills the first and removes the second. He is man enough to feel, God enough to forgive. His sympathy is untainted, His holiness unassailable. In Him, compassion is not corrupted by guilt but crowned with victory. He shares our nature without sharing our depravity. The priest of the Old Covenant stood at a distance, trembling before the Presence; this Priest enters boldly, bearing His own righteousness as the offering. The veil of separation falls before such a Mediator—torn from top to bottom, not by the hands of man, but by the hand of God. And the believer, once barred from the Holy of Holies, is now invited within: "Let us therefore come boldly unto the throne of grace" (4:16)—a summons unthinkable under Moses, but made possible through the mercy of a sinless Priest whose own blood opened the way everlasting.

The Divine Appointment

(Hebrews 5:4 – 10)

Priesthood is not a matter of human ambition. "No man taketh this honour unto himself, but he that is called of God, as was Aaron" (Heb. 5:4). The ministry of intercession is never seized—it is received. Holy office is not a career to be pursued but a calling to be bestowed. When men intrude into what God reserves for His own choosing, judgment follows swiftly. Israel learned this in the wilderness when Korah, Dathan, and Abiram rose up in rebellion, saying, "Ye take too much upon you, seeing all the congregation are holy" (Num. 16:3). They imagined that proximity to the camp meant equality before the altar. But God

Himself had drawn the boundary. The priesthood was not a public right—it was a divine trust. Moses answered, "The Lord will shew who are his, and who is holy" (Num. 16:5). When the morning came, the ground itself bore witness. The earth opened her mouth and swallowed the rebels alive. The censers they had dared to wave before the Lord were beaten into plates to cover the altar—a perpetual reminder that self-appointed worship ends in self-destruction. Self-appointment in sacred things provokes divine judgment. The God who calls is also the God who consumes; His service may not be claimed by presumption but entered only by grace.

Christ, though eternal Son, did not grasp the office by presumption. The Father appointed Him:

Thou art my Son, to day have I begotten thee (Ps. 2:7),

Thou art a priest for ever after the order of Melchizedek (Ps. 110:4).

Sonship and priesthood converge in Him. The same voice that declared, "Thou art my Son, this day have I begotten thee" (Ps. 2:7), also proclaimed, "Thou art a priest for ever after the order of Melchizedek" (Ps. 110:4). In these two divine decrees, heaven joined what earth could never unite—kingship and priesthood, deity and humanity, sovereignty and sympathy. His divine right flows not from lineage but from life eternal. The Levitical order traced descent through Aaron; holiness in that system was inherited by bloodline, confirmed by genealogy, and ended by death. When a priest died, his priesthood died with him.

But the order of Melchizedek depends upon no genealogy at all. Melchizedek appears in Scripture without record of father or mother, "without beginning of days or end of life" (Heb. 7:3), so that the silence of the text might speak the substance of the type. He stands alone in sacred history—without origin noted, without successor named—pointing beyond himself to a Priest whose existence cannot be measured in generations. What the Levitical line transmitted by descent, Christ possesses by divine essence. His priesthood is not inherited but inherent, not temporal but eternal. Melchizedek serves as shadow; Christ, the substance. The king of Salem foreshadows the Prince of Peace, and the priest of the Most High God prefigures the Son who is Himself the Most High.

During His earthly ministry, the Son demonstrated His priestly heart through obedience in suffering. Scripture records that He "offered up prayers and supplications with strong crying and tears unto him that was able to save him from death, and was heard in that he feared" (Heb. 5:7). These words pull back the veil of Gethsemane. There we see not a reluctant Redeemer, but a submissive Son. The garden's shadows reveal the cost of intercession. The One who could calm seas with a word now trembles beneath the tide of wrath about to break upon Him. His sweat falls like blood, His voice shakes heaven, and yet He says, "Nevertheless not my will, but thine, be done" (Luke 22:42). The Gethsemane agony reveals not weakness but willingness. It was not the fear of death that wrung tears from His eyes, but the weight of sin He would bear. The spotless Lamb was preparing to become sin for us, that we might be made the righteousness of God in Him.

"Though he were a Son, yet learned he obedience by the things which he suffered" (Heb. 5:8). The eternal Son, who had never known submission as incarnate flesh, entered into it fully. Learning obedience does not suggest former disobedience—it means that the Son experienced obedience in its severest form. What He had eternally willed as God, He now endured as man. Omnipotence learned dependence; the Creator learned what it meant to trust the Father while feeling forsaken. Every pang of pain, every humiliation, every mockery became the schoolroom of sympathy. Through suffering He was not made morally better but *perfected*—that is, brought to the full fitness of His office as High Priest. He who had always possessed the heart to save now possessed the experience to intercede.

Having thus obeyed unto death—even the death of the cross—He became the "author of eternal salvation unto all them that obey him" (Heb. 5:9). Salvation is not merely something He provided; it is something He authored. The cross is His signature written in blood upon the covenant of grace. Every pang He endured became ink upon that eternal page. The priest who wept in Gethsemane now reigns in glory, not as one broken by suffering but as one perfected through it. In every tear of Christ, the believer finds the assurance that his own tears are known, measured, and ministered by a High Priest who has felt their sting and triumphed through their pain.

The Aaronic priests ministered under temporary commission; Christ ministers under eternal consecration. He was called of God "an high priest after the order of Melchizedek" (5:10)—a priesthood both royal and righteous, kingly and compassionate, transcending tribal borders and temporal bounds.

The Need for Maturity

(Hebrews 5:11 – 6:3)

The writer interrupts his exposition to lament the spiritual sluggishness of his hearers. "Of whom we have many things to say, and hard to be uttered, seeing ye are dull of hearing" (5:11). The truths of Christ's priesthood are not obscure by nature; they are weighty, requiring exercised senses. Immaturity in the Word dulls discernment.

The believers addressed had long professed faith, yet remained untrained. They had heard the gospel, received its truth, and even defended it—but had not grown in it. "For when for the time ye ought to be teachers, ye have need that one teach you again which be the first principles of the oracles of God" (Heb. 5:12). They lingered among the alphabet of grace while the grammar of glory waited. They knew the syllables of salvation but had never learned to speak in the mature language of holiness. Faith had been confessed, but not cultivated. They could repeat doctrine, but they had not yet discerned how to apply it to their lives.

Milk is for babes—nourishment, yes, but insufficient for those called to endurance. The child may live on milk, but the soldier cannot fight on it. "Strong meat belongeth to them that are of full age... who by reason of use have their senses exercised to discern both good and evil" (5:14). The Christian life demands such exercise. Muscles of discernment do not develop by accident; they are strengthened in the gymnasium of obedience. Truth that is known but not practiced soon dulls the conscience. To hear without heeding is to harden the heart one sermon at a time. The writer does not chide them for infancy once—it is natural to begin with milk—but for remaining there long after they should have grown. God's design is not perpetual childhood but progressive maturity.

Therefore, he exhorts them to "leave the principles of the doctrine of Christ"—not to forsake them, but to build upon them—and go on unto perfection (6:1). Foundations are meant to bear walls; beginnings are meant to produce continuance. The same gospel that saves also summons us onward. The call to maturity is not a call away from Christ, but deeper into Him. The high priesthood of Christ is not for the indolent; it is for those pressing into the holy place with understanding hearts—believers who desire not only to be forgiven by His blood but to be fashioned by His hand. Christianity that remains content with infancy misrepresents its Priest. He who learned obedience through suffering now calls His people to learn obedience through surrender. Maturity, then, is not the luxury of a few but the duty of all who have been invited into the sanctuary of His grace.

The Greatness of Melchizedek's Order

Hebrews 7

The figure of Melchizedek stands as both type and testimony. He steps onto the stage of Scripture for only a moment, yet his shadow stretches across eternity. We meet him in Genesis 14, after Abram's rescue of Lot and victory over the confederate kings. As the patriarch returns from battle, weary but triumphant, he is met by a stranger—Melchizedek king of Salem, priest of the most high God (Gen. 14:18). Without introduction, this royal priest brings forth bread and wine, symbols of refreshment and communion, and blesses Abram in the name of the most high God, possessor of heaven and earth. Abram, recognizing divine authority, bows and gives him tithes of all.

This brief encounter becomes a revelation. "The lesser is blessed of the greater" (Heb. 7:7); therefore Melchizedek's priesthood both precedes and surpasses that of Levi. When Abraham bowed before this priest, Levi bowed in him; when Abraham offered tithes, the Levitical order paid tribute within his loins. Before Sinai was given, before Aaron was called, before the tabernacle was built, there already existed a priesthood independent of the law, older than the nation, and recognized by the Father of the Faithful himself. Its origin was not tribal but heavenly. Its sphere was not Israel but all nations. Its character was not ceremonial but spiritual.

Thus Melchizedek stands as a living prophecy: a priest who is also a king, a ruler who blesses rather than conquers, a man without recorded beginning or end. His silence in genealogy becomes eloquent in meaning. He is no mythic phantom but a foreshadowing reality—his very obscurity designed by God to prefigure One greater still. In Melchizedek we glimpse the outline; in Christ we behold the fulfillment. The mysterious king of Salem points to the Prince of Peace, whose priesthood needs no lineage and whose blessing needs no limit. Melchizedek's name means "King of Righteousness," and his title "King of Salem" means "King of Peace." In one person, righteousness and peace meet—a portrait only Christ fulfills. The Levitical system separated the crown from the ephod; no man could be both king and priest. But Christ unites them eternally.

The order of Melchizedek differs from the order of Aaron in three crucial ways:

1. **It is universal.** Melchizedek was a Gentile priest, unconnected to Israel's covenant. His appearance signals that divine mediation is not confined to one nation. Christ, therefore, is the High Priest for all peoples.

2. **It is perpetual.** The Aaronic office ended with death; new priests arose continually.   But Melchizedek is recorded "without beginning of days nor end of life" (7:3)—a deliberate silence pointing to an unending ministry.   So Christ "continueth ever and has an unchangeable priesthood" (7:24).

3. **It is perfect.** The law made men priests who had infirmity; the oath of God appointed the Son, "who is consecrated for evermore" (7:28).

Hence the conclusion:

Wherefore he is able also to save them to the uttermost that come unto God by him, seeing he ever liveth to make intercession for them (7:25).

No barrier remains of bloodline, ritual, or mortality. The intercession of Jesus is continual, effectual, and personal.   Every believer lives beneath the benediction of a living Priest.

The Better Covenant

Hebrews 8

If the priesthood changes, so must the covenant it administers.   The Levitical covenant engraved commandments upon stone; the New Covenant engraves obedience upon the heart. The Old Covenant could command righteousness but could not create it. It could restrain behavior but not renew desire. Tablets of stone could regulate conduct; they could never regenerate character. Under Moses, the law stood over the people; under Christ, the law lives within them.

Quoting Jeremiah 31:33, the writer declares:

I will put my laws into their mind, and write them in their hearts: and I will be to them a God, and they shall be to me a people (Heb. 8:10).

This is the miracle of the New Covenant. God does not merely give new directions—He produces new desires. The heart, in Scripture, is not the seat of emotion but the seat of the will. It is where choices are made, where loyalties are set, where the battle between flesh and spirit is decided. The Old Covenant could tell the heart what to do; the New Covenant transforms what the heart wants to do. Grace reaches deeper than commandment, shaping the will until obedience becomes delight.

The covenant is internal, moral, and spiritual. It does not abolish the old but fulfills it. The outward law restrained conduct; the inward law renews character.

The first governed from fear; the second governs from love. The first demanded righteousness; the second imparts it. The same voice that thundered from Sinai now whispers within the believer, not as a threat but as a presence. What once demanded conformity now imparts capacity. The God who wrote on stone now writes on spirit, and the heart once hardened by sin becomes the tablet of divine grace.

The Old Covenant depended upon repeated sacrifices and a human mediator; the new depends upon a finished sacrifice and a divine Mediator. Under the law, reconciliation was a process—daily offerings, yearly atonements, endless blood upon an endless altar. The priest stood because his work could never be completed. The smoke rose, the lamb fell, the conscience remained unclean.

The altar itself bore witness to that incompleteness. Made of acacia wood overlaid with bronze, it endured constant flame. Scripture commanded, "The fire shall ever be burning upon the altar; it shall never go out" (Lev. 6:13).   Hour after hour, generation after generation, the fire consumed flesh and fat until the bronze itself began to glow.   In the dim hours of evening, that faint red shimmer could be seen from the courts—a dull, trembling reminder that sin still demanded blood, that guilt still smoldered before God. The heat that devoured the sacrifice was the visible sermon of divine wrath.   Looking toward

Jerusalem, Israel saw not a beacon of peace but the glow of judgment delayed, not destroyed.

But at Calvary the scene changed. The dull glow of guilt's reminder was swallowed by the blazing light of grace's justification. The altar of bronze gave way to the cross of wood; the perpetual fire found its rest in the Lamb who offered Himself once for all. Christ is not a negotiator reconciling two parties at variance; He is the medium Himself—the living means by which reconciliation is wrought. A negotiator moves between two sides; a Mediator like Christ becomes the meeting place of both. In His body, heaven and earth meet; in His blood, justice and mercy embrace. The holiness that condemns and the grace that redeems are joined in perfect harmony at the cross.

Thus He obtained a more excellent ministry, not by altering the law but by fulfilling it. The altar that once glowed with continual flame has been eclipsed by the radiance of a finished redemption. "By how much also he is the mediator of a better covenant, which was established upon better promises" (Heb. 8:6). The light that once flickered with guilt now shines forever with grace, for the wrath that burned against sin has been quenched in the blood of the Son.

The handwriting of ordinances is taken away, nailed to the cross. What was shadow in Sinai becomes substance in Calvary. The believer's obedience now flows from renewed will, not from external

108

compulsion. God's law, inscribed upon the heart, shapes desire as well as duty.

The Greater Tabernacle and the Greater Sacrifice

Hebrews 9:1 – 15

He did not approach a manmade altar, nor minister in a temple of earth. He entered the true tabernacle, the dwelling of God Himself, and there presented His own blood. The glow of the Old Covenant altar was the reflection of wrath restrained; the radiance of the risen Christ is the light of redemption released. In Him, the shadow of judgment is overtaken by the dawn of grace. The altar once gleamed with borrowed light; the Lamb now shines with uncreated glory.

If the blood of bulls and goats could cleanse the flesh for a moment, "how much more shall the blood of Christ, who through the eternal Spirit offered himself without spot to God, purge your conscience from dead works to serve the living God" (9:14). The old fire purified the surface; the new flame purges the soul. The altar burned to remind; the cross stood to remove. In the earthly court, the glow of guilt was constant; in the heavenly court, the light of grace is eternal.

Here the writer gives Him a name that gathers all of this together: Mediator—Greek μεσίτης (*mesitēs*)—literally, the middle one, or the medium itself. A mediator in modern thought stands between two sides, carrying messages, seeking compromise. But the word used here is richer and deeper. Christ is not merely the messenger of peace—He is the medium in which peace was made. There is no negotiation between the holiness of God and the rebellion of man. We have nothing to offer, and God has nothing to give up. Sin cannot bargain with righteousness, and righteousness cannot lower its standard to meet sin halfway. The gulf cannot be bridged by dialogue—it must be spanned by death. Therefore Christ did not come to discuss atonement; He came to *be* atonement. He did not bring reconciliation as something He carried; He became reconciliation itself. In Him, divine wrath and human guilt met—and both were satisfied. His very body was the meeting ground between divine justice and human sin. His flesh was the veil rent, His blood the ink in which the covenant was signed, His life the living substance through which God and man were made one.

Therefore He is not simply between God and man; He is the place where God and man meet. He is the *mesitēs*, the medium through which grace flows, the living tabernacle where heaven and earth are joined. The old mediator spoke for man before God; the new Mediator is God come down to man. In His death, He stood in the gap; in His resurrection, He became the bridge itself.

The sacrifice that once demanded daily tending has been swallowed up in one eternal offering. The altar that once glowed with the memory of sin now shines as the testimony of salvation. The fire that never went out has finally found its resting place—in the heart of God's Son. The light that once warned of judgment now welcomes the redeemed. What once illuminated guilt now radiates grace. The bronze shimmer of atonement unfinished has been replaced by the brilliance of redemption complete.

Summary

The tabernacle of Israel was a shadow, not the substance. Its golden lampstand, its table of shewbread, its altar and veil—all were patterns of a greater reality. Year by year the high priest entered the holiest place with blood not his own, confessing by that act the insufficiency of all such offerings. The way into the holiest was not yet revealed while the first tabernacle stood. In Christ, that veil was torn; the shadow met the substance. He entered not into a sanctuary made with hands, but into heaven itself, now to appear in the presence of God for us.

The Mediator is not a negotiator standing between two parties, seeking compromise; He is the medium—

the divine substance in which reconciliation is wrought. There is no bargaining between holiness and rebellion. Man has nothing to offer; God has nothing to yield. The cross is not a table of peace talks but an altar of substitution. In His own blood Christ established the New Covenant, cleansing not the symbols but the conscience, and opening the living way into the presence of God. All that was hinted in the earthly service is fulfilled in Him—the true tabernacle, the eternal Priest, and the once-for-all sacrifice.

Application

To know Christ as Mediator is to rest from self-effort. The believer no longer carries offerings of merit or tears to the altar, but enters boldly by a finished work. Our worship is no longer bound to place or ritual; it is a heart drawn near by His blood. Every attempt to negotiate with God through good works, guilt, or religious performance denies the sufficiency of the cross. Faith confesses that Christ is enough.

- **Rest in the finished work.** We are not saved by negotiation but by substitution. Christ did not broker peace—He became our peace. Every attempt to earn, deserve, or maintain favor through effort denies the completeness of His cross.

- **Approach God with confidence.** The veil is gone. The believer stands in the presence of God not by worthiness but by the worth of the Lamb. Prayer and worship flow from relationship, not ritual.

- **Reject religious self-reliance.** Guilt, performance, and penance cannot cleanse the conscience. Only the blood of Christ reaches that deep. The heart that trusts Him alone is the one truly free to serve.

- **Let gratitude replace guilt.** Service becomes joy when it springs from acceptance rather than striving. Ministry is not payment rendered but thanksgiving offered.

- **Keep your eyes on the Mediator.** When conscience condemns or the accuser whispers, fix your gaze on Christ. He ever lives to intercede, and His presence is our assurance that the way remains open.

- **Live as a priest in the true tabernacle.** Wherever a believer stands becomes holy ground. The church, the home, the quiet place of prayer— all are sanctuaries when entered through Him.

Prayer

Father,

We thank You for the Mediator, the true Tabernacle in whom heaven and earth are joined.

We confess that we had nothing to offer, and You have nothing to yield, yet in Your mercy You gave Your own Son to stand where we could not stand.

Teach us to rest in His finished work. When our hearts condemn us, remind us that the veil is rent. When our labors weary us, remind us that access has already been granted.

Let our service rise not from guilt, but from gratitude; not from fear, but from faith.

Keep our eyes upon the Mercy Seat—Christ Himself— and let every prayer, every act of worship, be mingled with the blood that speaks better things than Abel.

Draw us near, and keep us near, until faith becomes sight in the holiest of all.

In Jesus' name, Amen.

5

Once for All: The Greatest Sacrifice

Hebrews 10 has often been called the salad chapter of the Bible, because it's filled with holy "let us." It's a fitting nickname, because this chapter gathers up all the truths of the previous nine and serves them in a practical dish that nourishes faith and obedience.

After nine chapters unveiling Christ's supremacy—His better revelation, His better covenant, and His better priesthood—the writer turns the corner. The long corridors of doctrine open into a living room of devotion. He invites us to act on what we've heard:

Let us draw near.

Let us hold fast.

Let us consider one another.

These are not cold commands; they are the natural responses of hearts awakened by grace. The believer who has seen the majesty of Christ cannot remain passive. Revelation calls for reaction. Truth demands transformation.

Doctrine now becomes duty, and revelation matures into response.

If Hebrews 1–9 tells us what Christ has done, then Hebrews 10 tells us what we must do because He has done it.

The first nine chapters lift our eyes to behold Him—enthroned above angels, greater than Moses, eternal High Priest of a better covenant. Chapter ten calls us to enter in—to live within the reality He has secured. Theology moves from the study to the sanctuary, from theory to practice, from the mind to the heart.

The gospel is not meant to be admired like a painting, but applied like a promise. It is truth meant to be walked in, prayed through, and lived out. The same Christ who tore the veil now calls us through it.

The Law's Shadow and the True Image (10:1–4)

The chapter opens with a sharp contrast:

"For the law having a shadow of good things to come, and not the very image of the things, can never... make the comers thereunto perfect."

The law was a shadow—an outline cast backward from Christ. Every commandment, every ceremony, every drop of priestly blood pointed toward Him, but none could produce Him. The tabernacle, the priesthood, the sacrifices—each was a silhouette of something better, something solid, something still to come.

A shadow cannot cleanse the conscience. It hints at substance but holds no power of its own. It may reveal form, but not fullness; movement, but not life. The law could show man what holiness looked like, yet could not make him holy. It could expose sin, but never erase it.

The sacrifices of bulls and goats were temporary scaffolding, not the finished temple. They propped up a people under covenant, but they could not bridge the gap between guilt and God. Every slain animal

was a faint echo of the sin still crouching at the door—
a yearly reminder that sin remained unpaid, that
judgment still hung overhead, that another sacrifice
would soon be needed.

Each altar proclaimed both man's sinfulness and
heaven's patience. God allowed the blood to flow not
because He was satisfied, but because He was
waiting. Those repeated sacrifices were placeholders
of grace—tokens of a promise not yet fulfilled. The
priest's hands never stayed clean, the fire never went
out, and the conscience never found rest.

Year after year the ritual repeated, like an unfinished
song returning to its first note: "You will need another
one tomorrow.

"The Willing Son (10:5–10)

Into that endless rhythm of sacrifice steps a single
voice—the voice of the Son.

> *"Wherefore when He cometh into the world, He
> saith, Sacrifice and offering Thou wouldest not,
> but a body hast Thou prepared Me."*

All the rivers of blood flowing from the altars of Israel
could never wash away sin. They testified to man's

failure, not his forgiveness. The repetition itself was proof that redemption was not yet accomplished. Heaven was not looking for more sacrifices—it was waiting for one.

The ancient worshipper could never forget the cost of sin. The temple was not a quiet place. It was filled with the smell of burning flesh and blood. The air hung heavy with smoke. The bleating of lambs and the lowing of oxen mingled with the chants of priests. The stones ran red. Death was everywhere.

It was a gruesome reminder that sin always brings death — and that forgiveness is never cheap. The law's sacrifices were not meant to sanitize sin, but to expose its horror. Each slain animal was a living picture of divine justice: the innocent suffering for the guilty, the pure cut down so the defiled might live another day.

Day after day, the people watched the knife rise and fall. They smelled the blood and felt the heat of the fire. And still it was not enough. Each sacrifice cried out that sin's debt was deeper than blood could pay — that something more, someone more, must come.

When Christ entered the world, He stepped willingly into that scene. He became not the priest holding the knife, but the Lamb on the altar. The One who gave the law bore the law's curse. The hands that formed

Adam became the hands that were pierced for Adam's race.

The eternal Word took on a body, not as another priest among many, but as the final offering itself. The Son did not enter the world reluctantly or under compulsion. He came willingly, joyfully, obediently—saying, "Lo, I come (in the volume of the book it is written of Me) to do Thy will, O God." *(Heb. 10:7)*

That single statement divides all history. Every burnt offering and meal offering, every peace offering and trespass offering, every drop of blood under the law converged in that moment. The shadows gave way to substance. The altar met its answer.

"He taketh away the first", the writer says, "that He may establish the second." (Heb. 10:9)

Christ brought an end to the old system not by rejection but by fulfillment. He didn't break the law—He completed it. He didn't abolish the sacrifices—He embodied them. In His obedience, every type and figure found its meaning.

By that will—His will, perfectly aligned with the Father's—"we are sanctified through the offering of the body of Jesus Christ once for all."

Not year by year.

Not morning and evening.

Not again and again.

Once. For all.

The priests of old stood before their altars, hands red with borrowed blood, knowing another lamb would soon be needed. But when Christ stretched out His hands on the cross, it was not the blood of another—it was His own. The Creator allowed Himself to be slain by His creation so that sinners might be sanctified forever.

He who had no sin bore sin's full sentence. He who never tasted guilt drank guilt's bitter cup to the dregs. He, who owed no death, willingly embraced ours. He died the death we had earned so that we might live the life He deserves.

What greater obedience could there be? What greater love could God display?

The cross was not a tragic accident—it was a deliberate act of divine will. The altar of Calvary was the meeting place of two eternal purposes: the Father's justice and the Son's mercy. And in that moment, heaven's will and earth's need became one.

The sacrifices of law said, "Do."

The sacrifice of Christ says, "Done."

The Seated Priest (10:11–14)

When the writer says, "Every priest standeth daily ministering and offering oftentimes the same sacrifices, which can never take away sins," (Heb. 10:11) he is describing exhaustion. The tabernacle never slept. Morning and evening, year after year, the fire burned, the blood flowed, and the priests stood. There were no benches, no resting places, no intermissions. Their ministry was endless because their offering was endless.

The absence of a chair in the Holy Place was itself a sermon. There was a table for the showbread, a lampstand for light, an altar for incense, an ark for testimony—but no seat. Why? Because the work was never done. The priest could not sit while sin remained.

But "this Man"—and how the writer loves that phrase—"this Man, after He had offered one sacrifice for sins forever, sat down on the right hand of God." (Heb. 10:12)

When Jesus cried, "It is finished," the world shook because heaven agreed. He did not merely pause— He sat down. The posture of heaven's priest declared what the altar had accomplished: the work is complete, the debt is canceled, the curse is lifted.

To sit at the right hand of God means more than rest —it means **reign**. He is not merely relieved of labor;

122

He is enthroned in victory. The cross was not His defeat but His coronation. The thorns became His crown, and the wood became His throne.

Every other priest stood between two fires—the fire of sacrifice and the fire of conscience—always aware that the blood on his hands could never cleanse his own heart. But Christ entered once into the true sanctuary, not with the blood of others, but with His own. And when He emerged, the smoke of wrath was gone, replaced by the fragrance of reconciliation.

Now He waits—not because His work is incomplete, but because history is. "From henceforth expecting till His enemies be made His footstool." (Heb. 10:13). The cross secured the victory; time merely awaits its unveiling.

And when that day comes—when the last enemy is under His feet, when the trumpet sounds and the kingdom of this world becomes the kingdom of our Lord and of His Christ—we will stand beside Him, not as servants trembling at the altar, but as sons rejoicing at the throne.

A Law Written on the Heart (10:15–18)

The writer now reminds us that the Holy Ghost Himself testifies to the reality of this New Covenant:

"Whereof the Holy Ghost also is a witness to us: for after that He had said before, This is the covenant that I will make with them after those days, saith the Lord, I will put My laws into their hearts, and in their minds will I write them; And their sins and iniquities will I remember no more." (Heb. 10:15-17)

This is the heartbeat of grace. The same Spirit who once engraved the law upon tablets of stone now engraves it upon the living tablet of the heart. The handwriting of Sinai, which condemned, has become the inscription of Calvary, which redeems.

An external law can restrain the hand, but only an internal law can renew the heart. The law written on stone could command obedience, but it could not create it. Only the Spirit can take the will that once resisted God and make it love His ways.

Paul describes this miracle in another place:

"Ye are manifestly declared to be the epistle of Christ ministered by us, written not with ink, but with the Spirit of the living God; not in tables of stone, but in fleshy tables of the heart." (2 Corinthians 3:3)

Before Christ, we were like Paul in his pre-conversion zeal—wanting to do right, but doing wrong; desiring holiness, yet enslaved to self. Romans 7 paints that painful picture:

"For the good that I would I do not: but the evil which I would not, that I do." (Romans 7:19)

Then comes the cry:

"O wretched man that I am! who shall deliver me from the body of this death?" (Romans 7:24)

And the triumphant answer:

"I thank God through Jesus Christ our Lord." (Romans 7:25)

Through the cross, the Spirit of God takes that desperate heart and engraves upon it a new desire. No longer, "I must obey," but "I long to please Him." This is sanctification in its truest sense—not behavior imposed from without, but love written within.

The law of Christ is not a leash but a lifeline. It binds us, not by compulsion, but by affection. The same hand that once thundered from Sinai now writes softly upon the believer's soul, shaping every thought and bending every desire toward holiness.

And the promise continues:

> *"Their sins and iniquities will I remember no more." (Hebrews 10:17)*

What an exchange—law inscribed, sin erased. The first covenant carved condemnation into stone; the New Covenant carves forgiveness into the heart. God Himself chooses amnesia regarding our failures. The blood of Christ doesn't merely cover sin; it cancels the record.

The writer concludes,

> *"Now where remission of these is, there is no more offering for sin." (Hebrews 10:18)*

There is nothing left to pay, nothing left to prove, nothing left to add. The ledger is clear. The handwriting of ordinances that was against us has been nailed to the cross (Colossians 2:14).

God's justice is satisfied, His mercy magnified, His promise fulfilled. The law that once stood over us now lives within us, and the heart that once rebelled now beats in rhythm with its Redeemer.

The Helmet of Salvation

Hebrews 10:16 linked with Romans 8:5–6; Ephesians 6:17

When God writes His law upon the heart, He does not stop there—He also renews the mind. The heart is the fountain of desire, but the mind is the gate through which every thought and influence must pass. A transformed heart calls for a guarded mind.

Paul describes that transformation in his letter to the Romans. After the cry of despair in chapter 7—"O wretched man that I am! who shall deliver me from the body of this death?" (Romans 7:24)—the first words of chapter 8 answer the cry with thunderous hope:

"There is therefore now no condemnation to them which are in Christ Jesus." (Romans 8:1)

The same man who once found himself enslaved to the law of sin and death now rejoices that "the law of the Spirit of life in Christ Jesus hath made me free" (Romans 8:2). Freedom in the Spirit is not freedom from thought—it is freedom unto right thinking.

Paul calls this the difference between the carnal and the spiritual mind:

"For they that are after the flesh do mind the things of the flesh; but they that are after the Spirit the things of the Spirit. For to be carnally minded is death; but to be spiritually minded is life and peace." (Romans 8:5–6)

That "spiritual mind" is the same reality Hebrews 10 describes when God says, "I will put My laws into their hearts, and in their minds will I write them." (Hebrews 10:16) The law written within becomes the lens through which we see without. The Spirit-engraved heart now educates the redeemed mind.

Paul later calls this safeguard "the helmet of salvation" (Ephesians 6:17)—a picture of protection and perspective. A soldier may have every weapon polished and ready, but without his helmet he is one blow away from ruin. So too, the believer without a renewed mind is one lie away from despair.

Through the Word of God, the Spirit trains our thoughts to run in holy channels. Every truth we receive, every influence we allow, every decision we make must pass beneath the helmet's guard. "Garbage in, garbage out" is more than a computer maxim—it is a spiritual reality. The unrenewed mind cannot produce the fruits of righteousness.

We cannot feed our minds with the world's corruption and expect heaven's peace to rule within. The songs we hum, the screens we watch, the words we speak

—all of it enters the sanctuary of thought. What the mind receives, the life reflects.

That is why the Spirit writes upon both heart and mind. The heart directs toward what the mind knows, and the mind guards what the heart treasures. Together they form the inner sanctuary of the believer —the place where truth is enthroned and lies find no lodging.

Christianity does not silence reason; it sanctifies it. The first act of the Spirit upon a believing soul is not to make it mystical but to make it sane. The world calls faith blindness, yet without faith the mind remains darkened. The gospel restores reason by restoring relationship—the creature once estranged now thinks again with his Creator.

So we put on the helmet of salvation daily, not as ornament but as armor. We take "every thought captive to the obedience of Christ" (2 Corinthians 10:5). We test every idea by the Word. We let the cross filter our affections and the resurrection steady our hope. And as we do, the Spirit keeps our minds sound, our hearts steady, and our steps sure.

For to be spiritually minded is still, in every age, "life and peace." (Romans 8:6)

Sins Remembered No More

Hebrews 10:17–18

"And their sins and iniquities will I remember no more." (Hebrews 10:17)

Those are among the most astonishing words ever uttered by God.

He who forgets nothing chooses to forget. He who sees all chooses to turn His eyes away. The Judge of all the earth, who misses not a sparrow's fall nor a whisper in the dark, has decided that the record of His redeemed will never again be opened.

This is not divine absentmindedness—it is divine mercy. God does not lose information; He lays it aside under the blood. What justice once recorded, grace has now erased.

Under the Old Covenant, Israel's worshippers were never allowed to forget their sin. Every day the altar smoked. Every year the high priest entered again with blood that could only cover, never cleanse. Leviticus made remembering mandatory; Calvary made remembering unnecessary.

"But in those sacrifices there is a remembrance again made of sins every year. For it is not

possible that the blood of bulls and of goats should take away sins." (Hebrews 10:3–4)

The Day of Atonement came and went like a tolling bell—one more year of mercy, one more year of guilt postponed. But now, in Christ, that endless reminder has ended. The bell has fallen silent. The work that could never be finished is finished indeed.

"Now where remission of these is, there is no more offering for sin." (Hebrews 10:18)

Those are words of completion. The sacrificial system has no further business; the tabernacle's purpose has been fulfilled. The fire on the altar has met its final flame in the pierced hands of the Son of God.

This forgiveness is not partial or probationary. It is final, legal, eternal. The debt of sin has not been renegotiated; it has been paid. God's justice has not been relaxed; it has been satisfied. The sinner's record has not been sealed; it has been destroyed.

"As far as the east is from the west, so far hath He removed our transgressions from us." (Psalm 103:12)

"Thou wilt cast all their sins into the depths of the sea." (Micah 7:19)

These are not poetic exaggerations but covenantal guarantees. The cross stands as God's public declaration that sin's reign is over.

Still, we live in a world where sin's consequences linger. The forgiven addict may still bear the scars, the reconciled husband may still rebuild what sin broke, the redeemed sinner may still weep over what cannot be undone. Yet heaven's record shows none of it. The handwriting of ordinances that was against us has been nailed to the cross (Colossians 2:14). The stain that once cried out for vengeance has been washed away in crimson grace.

When God says, "I will remember no more," He means that the sin which once stood between us is gone forever. It will never be re-summoned as evidence, never re-entered as debt, never revived as accusation. The blood of Christ not only covers—it cancels. It not only atones—it abolishes.

For the believer, forgiveness is not a fragile truce but a permanent peace. We no longer approach God through ritual apology but through relational confidence. We come, not as servants seeking pardon, but as sons enjoying fellowship.

This is the glory of the New Covenant: the same God who once wrote our guilt in stone has now written our righteousness in His Son. And that record cannot be broken, altered, or undone.

Access into the Holiest

Hebrews 10:19–21

"Having therefore, brethren, boldness to enter into the holiest by the blood of Jesus,

by a new and living way, which He hath consecrated for us, through the veil, that is to say, His flesh;

and having an High Priest over the house of God." (Hebrews 10:19–21)

With those words, the letter moves from courtroom to throne room. The believer who has been justified by the blood now receives an invitation to draw near to the very presence of God. The altar has become a doorway. The cross has become a key.

In the tabernacle, there was always a barrier. A heavy veil separated the Holy Place from the Most Holy, where the ark of the covenant stood beneath the overshadowing wings of the cherubim. That thick curtain was more than fabric; it was theology woven into cloth. It declared that sinful man could not freely approach a holy God.

Once a year—only once—the high priest passed through that veil, trembling, bearing the blood of

133

atonement. The people watched from a distance, waiting to see if he would return alive. The sound of the golden bells on his robe was their assurance that the sacrifice had been accepted.

Then came the day of the cross. When Jesus cried out, "It is finished," (John 19:30) the earth shook, the rocks split, and the veil of the temple was torn in two from the top to the bottom (Matthew 27:51). God Himself took hold of that curtain and ripped it apart, as though to say, "The separation is over. The debt is paid. Come in."

That veil, the writer tells us, represented Christ's flesh:

> "by a new and living way, which He hath consecrated for us, through the veil, that is to say, His flesh." (Hebrews 10:20)

When His body was broken, the barrier was removed. His torn flesh became our open door. What had for centuries been a forbidden space has now become our dwelling place. We enter, not as trespassers, but as children welcomed home.

And we do not come alone. We come "having an High Priest over the house of God." (Hebrews 10:21)

Christ did not open the way merely to step aside and watch us go in—He entered with us and for us. He stands even now in the presence of the Father, representing us by name, pleading not with words but with wounds. The marks in His hands are our credentials. The scars in His side are our proof of purchase.

When we pray, we are not knocking at a closed door; we are walking through one that stands forever open. When we worship, we are not standing outside the curtain, hoping for access; we are seated in heavenly places in Christ Jesus (Ephesians 2:6).

This is what the writer calls "a new and living way." New—not in time alone, but in quality. The Greek word *prosphatos* carries the sense of something freshly slain and freshly opened. The way remains ever new, because the sacrifice remains ever living. Christ's blood does not congeal or decay; His atonement is as fresh today as the hour it was shed.

And it is living—because the One who died now lives forever. The Old Covenant offered access through death alone. The New Covenant offers it through the Living One who conquered death. Our approach to God is not through a lifeless ritual, but through a living Redeemer.

Therefore we come boldly—not arrogantly, but confidently. The blood gives us courage. The Son gives us welcome. The Spirit gives us words.

The holiest place is no longer a location in Jerusalem; it is a position in Christ. The temple curtain may hang in ruins, but the true sanctuary stands open in heaven. And every believer, no matter how ordinary, no matter how weak, has the right to walk in.

We enter not as priests by birthright, but as worshippers by new birth.

We stand, not outside the flame, but within the fellowship.

We pray, not beneath wrath, but beneath mercy.

The veil is gone. The way is open. The presence is near.

The blood that purchased pardon has also purchased access.

The "Let Us" Commands

Hebrews 10:22–25

Having opened the way into the holiest, the writer now invites us to walk through it. The doctrine becomes a doorway. The theology becomes a call to action.

> *"Let us draw near with a true heart in full assurance of faith, having our hearts sprinkled from an evil conscience, and our bodies washed with pure water.*

Let us hold fast the profession of our faith without wavering; (for He is faithful that promised;)

And let us consider one another to provoke unto love and to good works:

Not forsaking the assembling of ourselves together, as the manner of some is; but exhorting one another: and so much the more, as ye see the day approaching." (Hebrews 10:22–25)

The Holy Spirit piles these exhortations one upon another like stepping stones for the believer's walk. The invitation is corporate—let us. The faith of the New Covenant is not solitary; it is shared. The same blood that gives us access to God also binds us to one another.

1. Let Us Draw Near (v. 22)

The first response to grace is worship. Because the way is open, we must come.

Not cautiously, as though we were intruders, but confidently, as beloved children. We are invited to draw near "with a true heart in full assurance of faith."

A true heart means a sincere one—not divided, not pretending. God does not listen for perfect words but for honest ones. A heart that hides nothing is a heart He receives gladly.

And we come "in full assurance of faith." Faith is not a feeling but a resting. We rest in what Christ has already done. We don't bring a résumé of works, but a reliance upon grace.

The imagery of priestly preparation runs through this verse: "having our hearts sprinkled from an evil conscience, and our bodies washed with pure water." (v. 22)

Under the Old Covenant, priests were sprinkled with blood and washed at the laver before ministering in the sanctuary (Exodus 29:4, 20–21). The New Covenant believer approaches God in the same pattern—cleansed by blood, washed by the Word.

When we draw near, we do not track sin into the sanctuary. We come confessing, forsaking, cleansing our hearts before His holiness. To enter unprepared is to forget the cost of the access we've been given. We are welcomed freely, but we must come reverently.

2. Let Us Hold Fast (v. 23)

The second exhortation is to perseverance:

"Let us hold fast the profession of our faith without wavering; (for He is faithful that promised.)" (v. 23)

If "draw near" is about our approach, "hold fast" is about our endurance. The same faith that brings us into fellowship must keep us there.

To hold fast means to grip tightly what God has spoken. We cling to the promise, not the feeling. Our anchor is not in ourselves, but in the One who "is faithful that promised."

When the winds of doubt or the storms of culture beat against our confidence, we stand fast because He does not change. The faithfulness of Christ is the steel in the spine of the church.

This is why the believer must wear "the helmet of salvation" (Ephesians 6:17). A guarded mind sustains a steadfast heart. Every idea, every philosophy, every temptation must be tested against the truth of the gospel. We cannot live like the world and think like heaven; we must renew the mind daily.

Holding fast is not passive endurance—it is active fidelity. We live what we profess. We demonstrate in our choices what we declare in our creed. Our profession is not a slogan; it is a way of life.

3. Let Us Consider One Another (vv. 24–25)

Grace not only changes how we approach God—it changes how we approach people.

> *"And let us consider one another to provoke unto love and to good works:*
>
> *Not forsaking the assembling of ourselves together, as the manner of some is; but exhorting one another: and so much the more, as ye see the day approaching." (vv. 24–25)*

To consider means to think carefully, to take note, to look beyond ourselves. In the church, our attention must be mutual. We are not spectators but participants in one another's spiritual welfare.

The word provoke usually carries a negative sense, but here it is redeemed. We are to stir each other—not to anger, but to love; not to rivalry, but to good works. The true mark of spiritual maturity is not isolation but investment.

The next line is one of the most neglected commands in modern Christianity: "Not forsaking the assembling of ourselves together." (v. 25) The Greek word usually translated "church" (*ekklesia*) means "assembly." The church is not defined by architecture, hierarchy, or livestream—it is the people of God gathered in one place around one Lord.

From the beginning, believers met together to worship, to pray, to learn, and to serve. Christianity cannot be practiced in solitude. The body must be present to be a body.

To neglect gathering is to starve the soul. We need one another's prayers, one another's encouragement, one another's example. Isolation breeds apathy; fellowship fuels faith.

And this assembling is not optional or occasional—it becomes more urgent as the world grows darker: "and so much the more, as ye see the day approaching." The closer we draw to the return of Christ, the more vital our communion becomes. The church that gathers faithfully will stand firmly when the shaking comes.

The writer of Hebrews is not content with orthodoxy —he calls for **orthopraxy**. If Christ's work has opened the way, we must walk it. If His sacrifice has sanctified us, we must live as sanctified people. The faith that draws near must hold fast, and the heart that holds fast must love well.

> **Orthopraxy**
>
> Right practice; living out true belief through obedient action consistent with God's revealed truth.

The "let us" of Hebrews 10 is the language of family, not formality. It is the voice of pilgrims walking together toward the unshakable kingdom, urging one another onward, arm in arm, with eyes fixed on the King who waits at the end of the way.

The Warning and the Reward

Hebrews 10:26–39

Every open door brings with it a responsibility. The gospel's invitation is universal, but its response divides the hearers into three classes: **believers**, **assenters**, and **rejectors**.

- The **believer** has entered the holiest by the blood of Jesus, resting in the finished work of the cross.

- The **assenter** stands near the door, intellectually persuaded, even stirred in conscience, but never surrendered in heart.

- The **rejector** turns away, trampling the invitation underfoot and counting the blood that sanctified the church an unholy thing.

It is this last class—the **deliberate rejector**—that the writer now warns with trembling gravity:

"For if we sin wilfully after that we have received the knowledge of the truth, there remaineth no more sacrifice for sins,

But a certain fearful looking for of judgment and fiery indignation, which shall devour the adversaries." (Hebrews 10:26–27)

This "willful sin" is not the weakness of a believer, nor the hesitation of an assenter. It is the hardened defiance of one who knowingly rejects the gospel. It is to stand at the threshold of mercy, look upon the blood that opens the way, and refuse to enter. It is to prefer the outer court of self-effort to the inner sanctuary of grace.

The believer's failures are covered by the blood. The assenter's struggle still leaves room for repentance. But for the rejector—there is no other altar to turn to. "There remaineth no more sacrifice for sins." The temple of grace has but one Lamb; there will never be another.

The writer reminds them of the justice under the first covenant:

"He that despised Moses' law died without mercy under two or three witnesses." (v. 28)

If disobedience brought death under a temporary covenant written on stone, what shall be the end of those who scorn an eternal covenant written in blood?

> *"Of how much sorer punishment, suppose ye, shall he be thought worthy, who hath trodden under foot the Son of God, and hath counted the blood of the covenant, wherewith He was sanctified, an unholy thing, and hath done despite unto the Spirit of grace?" (v. 29)*

To tread underfoot the Son of God is to reject the only sacrifice that can save. To call the blood of Christ common is to despise the very price of redemption. To resist the Spirit of grace is to slam the door of heaven from the inside.

This is not the trembling of faith but the treachery of unbelief.

It is not a stumble along the way but a settled turning from the Way Himself.

- **For the believer,** this warning sobers but does not threaten. It reminds us that the blood we trust is holy and precious.

- **For the assenter,** it is a summons to decide—no longer to admire Christ from a distance but to fall before Him in repentance.

- **For the rejector,** it is a final plea before the flames —a last echo of mercy before the sound of judgment.

"For we know Him that hath said, Vengeance belongeth unto Me, I will recompense, saith the Lord. And again, The Lord shall judge His people.

It is a fearful thing to fall into the hands of the living God." (vv. 30–31)

These are not words of cruelty but of compassion. God's warnings are not meant to drive us away, but to draw us in. The hands of the living God are fearful to the rebel, but nail-scarred to the redeemed. The difference is not the character of the hands—but the covering of the blood.

The question is simple: **Is the blood on you, or under you?**

- The **believer** stands under the blood—sheltered.

- The **assenter** stands beside it—undecided.

- The **rejector** stands on it—trampling.

Only one of those positions is safe.

Then, as a faithful pastor, the writer turns from warning to encouragement. He will not leave trembling saints without assurance.

"But call to remembrance the former days, in which, after ye were illuminated, ye endured a great fight of afflictions;

Partly, whilst ye were made a gazingstock both by reproaches and afflictions; and partly, whilst ye became companions of them that were so used.

For ye had compassion of me in my bonds, and took joyfully the spoiling of your goods, knowing in yourselves that ye have in heaven a better and an enduring substance." (vv. 32–34)

He reminds them of their earlier faithfulness. They had suffered and endured. They had been publicly mocked for Christ's sake and had borne loss with joy, knowing they possessed something greater. Their past perseverance was evidence of present grace

"Cast not away therefore your confidence, which hath great recompence of reward." (v. 35)

Confidence here means assurance—settled conviction that Christ is enough, that His promise cannot fail, and His presence cannot leave. To throw it away is to cast aside the very anchor that secures the soul.

> "For ye have need of patience, that, after ye have done the will of God, ye might receive the promise." (v. 36)

Patience is the bridge between obedience and fulfillment. Every promise of God ripens in its season, and faith is the soil in which it matures.

Then the trumpet of hope sounds again:

> "For yet a little while, and He that shall come will come, and will not tarry." (v. 37)

The delay of Christ's return is not neglect but mercy. He waits that more might believe, that the gospel might gather its full harvest. Yet His coming is sure. He who came to redeem will come again to reign.

> "Now the just shall live by faith: but if any man draw back, My soul shall have no pleasure in him." (v. 38, quoting Habakkuk 2:4)

Here is the dividing line: the just live by faith; the faithless draw back. The righteous are not those who never falter, but those who never forsake. Faith may tremble, but it does not turn away.

And then the writer closes with one of the most hopeful declarations in all Scripture:

"But we are not of them who draw back unto perdition; but of them that believe to the saving of the soul." (v. 39)

That is the voice of assurance. The true believer is not of the shrinking kind, but of the steadfast kind. We may grow weary, but we do not walk away. We may face affliction, but we do not abandon our confession.

Faith holds on, not because of its own strength, but because of the strength of the One who holds it. The same hand that was pierced for us now preserves us.

We are not of them who draw back.

We are of them who believe.

And believing, we live—"to the saving of the soul."

Summary

Hebrews 10 gathers every truth of the epistle into one grand declaration: Christ's work is finished.

- The shadow has yielded to substance, the figure to the fulfillment.

- By one offering, He has perfected forever those who are sanctified.

- The law now lives within us, the veil is torn before us, and the High Priest intercedes beside us.

Therefore, the Christian life becomes one great "let us":

- Draw near.

- Hold fast.

- Consider one another.

Doctrine must now become devotion.

- If He has sat down, we must stand up.

- If He has entered in, we must draw near.

- If He has loved us, we must love one another.

Application

1. Let us draw near.

   - **Cultivate daily prayer.** God does not require eloquence—He desires honesty.

   - **Prepare your heart before entering His presence;** confess sin, seek cleansing, and come boldly.

   - **Remember:** when you pray, Jesus stands beside you with nail-scarred hands.

2. Let us hold fast.

   - **Live what you profess.** Your theology must shape your temperament.

   - **Guard your mind**—wear the helmet of salvation; filter all you take in through Christ.

   - **Stay anchored:** your High Priest is faithful that promised.

3. Let us consider one another.

   - **Reclaim the assembly:** church is people gathered, not hierarchy or building.

   - **Encourage, visit, and serve one another**—especially those absent or weary.

   - **Come not to be entertained**, but to edify.

- **Gather** so much the more as you see the Day approaching.

4. Let us not draw back.

- **There is no other sacrifice for sin;** cling to the one offered once for all.

- **Endure trials with patience**; your confidence has great reward.

- **Live as citizens of the unshakable Kingdom;** believing to the saving of the soul.

Prayer

Father,

we thank You for the once-for-all sacrifice of Your Son, for sins remembered no more, for a veil torn from top to bottom, for access into the holiest through His blood.

Engrave Your law upon our hearts, steady our faith when the world wavers, and teach us to draw near daily— to hold fast, to consider one another, and to live as those who truly believe it is finished.

In Jesus' name we pray,

Amen.

6

Faith That Sees the Unseen

The Definition of True Faith

Hebrews 11 is often called the faith chapter. It stands as a gallery of portraits—men and women who dared to act upon unseen truth. Yet before the writer begins to paint those portraits, he pauses to define what faith actually is.

> *"Now faith is the substance of things hoped for, the evidence of things not seen." (Hebrews 11:1)*

This single sentence shatters every modern misconception of faith. The world treats faith as a mood—a warm optimism, a vague assurance that "everything will be okay." We hear it constantly in conversation and pop culture: faith as emotion, faith as comfort, faith as self-generated hope. It sounds noble, but it is empty. Unanchored faith is not faith at all. It is optimism unmoored from truth, a pleasant delusion that cannot stand when the storm breaks. It is as dangerous as a reckless driver who speeds through warning signs, confident in his own skill, blind to the cliff ahead.

True faith—the faith described in Scripture—is anchored obedience. It does not invent its own reality; it cooperates with the reality God has spoken. The Greek word translated substance is *hypostasis*, meaning "that which stands under." It describes something solid, the unseen foundation that gives form to what stands upon it. Faith, then, is not an abstract wish. It is the believer's participation in the unchanging reality of God's Word. It takes what God has declared to be true and acts upon it, bringing the invisible truth into visible expression.

Faith is not imagination—it is manifestation. It does not create truth but responds to it. The believer's action does not cause God's Word to be true; it simply reveals that it already is. Every step of obedience aligns the visible world of human choice with the invisible order of divine decree.

When we act upon the Word of God, we are not leaping into the dark; we are stepping into the light that has been shining since creation. Faith is never irrational—it is simply operating by a higher rationality, one rooted in God's revelation rather than in human perception. The unseen is not unreal; it is simply unobserved. Faith lives from that deeper reality outward.

The author immediately grounds this truth in creation itself:

> "Through faith we understand that the worlds were framed by the word of God, so that things which are seen were not made of things which do appear." (v. 3)

Faith is not blind belief—it is enlightened understanding. The word understand here is vital: the world can observe creation, but only the mind renewed by faith can comprehend it. Unbelief sees patterns but cannot perceive purpose. It catalogs mechanisms yet misses the Mind behind them.

A saved mind—a mind awakened by faith—sees the same stars and seas that unbelief sees, but interprets them differently. It perceives design where others see chance, and order where others see accident. Faith does not close its eyes to reason; it redeems reason. It restores intellect to its rightful alignment with revelation.

155

That is why the writer says, through faith we understand. Without faith, understanding collapses into confusion. It is only by faith that we can accurately comprehend cosmology—the true order of the created world. The heavens declare the glory of God, but only the believing heart can hear the declaration.

History bears witness to this harmony between faith and true reason. Sir Isaac Newton, whose discoveries reshaped modern science, never saw conflict between scientific inquiry and divine revelation. His study of gravity, light, and motion was not an escape from faith but an expression of it. He wrote, "This most beautiful system of the sun, planets, and comets could only proceed from the counsel and dominion of an intelligent and powerful Being." For Newton, science was a window into the mind of God; the laws he discovered were evidence of the Logos who framed the worlds by His word.

Such is the fruit of a redeemed intellect. Faith restores the mind to its intended function—to think God's thoughts after Him. It rescues knowledge from chaos and binds wisdom to worship. Without faith, the world becomes a meaningless collection of data; with faith, it becomes a revelation of divine order.

To live by faith, then, is to live as one who sees reality correctly. The world's foundations are not chaos but covenant; its structure is not accident but artistry.

156

Faith understands that the visible arises from the invisible, that creation is upheld by the unseen Word of God. The saved mind recognizes that the cosmos is not self-existent but spoken—framed by the eternal decree of the Creator.

Faith Displayed in the Ancients

Beginning in verse 4, the writer leads us into a gallery of lives shaped by faith — the elders who "obtained a good report" not because they dreamed of better things, but because they acted upon divine truth. Each name in this chapter is a window into how invisible realities become visible through obedience. These are not legends or moral examples merely; they are demonstrations of faith's essence — human will submitted to God's Word.

The first portrait is Abel, whose faith shines against the darkness of a fallen world.

> *"By faith Abel offered unto God a more excellent sacrifice than Cain, by which he obtained witness that he was righteous, God testifying of his gifts: and by it he being dead yet speaketh." (v. 4)*

Abel's faith was not emotion — it was obedience to revelation. Though Scripture gives us few details, the

157

context of Genesis 4 suggests that both brothers knew the kind of offering God required. Cain brought the fruit of the ground — the work of his own hands. Abel brought a firstling of his flock and the fat thereof — a blood sacrifice, prefiguring the Lamb to come.

Here, faith makes the invisible visible. Abel's act gave visible form to the unseen principle of atonement: without shedding of blood is no remission. His faith did not invent righteousness; it responded to the righteousness God had already revealed. Through obedience, he entered into the unseen order of redemption.

In Cain, we see unanchored faith — sincerity without submission. He believed in God's existence but not in God's way. His sacrifice was earnest but disobedient, and therefore empty. Abel, by contrast, believed that God's Word meant what it said. His offering testified that sin cannot be covered by the sweat of man's labor, only by the life of another. Faith acted, and in acting, revealed the invisible mercy of God.

That is why the writer says, "By it he being dead yet speaketh." The faith that obeys still testifies long after the believer's voice has fallen silent. Abel's altar became a sermon — a declaration that salvation is not achieved by works but received by trust. His faith brought eternal truth into the temporal world; his obedience gave shape to the unseen gospel.

158

The next portrait is Enoch, a man who disappeared not by death but by divine invitation.

"By faith Enoch was translated that he should not see death; and was not found, because God had translated him: for before his translation he had this testimony, that he pleased God." (v. 5)

In Abel we see faith worshiping — trusting the unseen principle of atonement.

In Enoch we see faith walking — living daily in unseen fellowship.

The world of Enoch's day was corrupt and violent, a world rapidly ripening for judgment. Yet amid that decay, one man walked with God. The Hebrew word for "walked" in Genesis 5:24 conveys continuous motion — habitual communion. Faith was not a momentary emotion for Enoch; it was a lifelong direction. His steps became visible evidence of invisible companionship.

He did not measure faith by what he felt, but by whom he followed. While others followed their desires, Enoch ordered his life by the unseen presence of God. Every choice, every path, every quiet decision revealed the reality of that fellowship. And when his walk was complete, God simply took him home. Faith made eternal life visible — a mortal man vanishing into immortality.

The text says he "pleased God." That phrase defines what faith really is: not human optimism toward heaven, but divine approval toward man. Faith delights God because it recognizes His truth as more real than circumstance. Enoch's life pleased God because he lived as though God were visibly at his side. He did not see, yet he walked as though he did — and thus faith turned the unseen into reality.

The writer then adds,

> *"But without faith it is impossible to please Him: for he that cometh to God must believe that He is, and that He is a rewarder of them that diligently seek Him." (v. 6)*

This verse exposes the absolute necessity of faith. It is not one spiritual gift among others; it is the foundation of all true relationship with God. Without faith, there is no pleasing Him, because unbelief denies His existence or mistrusts His character. Faith begins with belief that He is — not merely that He exists, but that His being defines all being. It continues in confidence that He rewards those who seek Him — that His unseen favor is more substantial than visible reward.

Enoch's translation becomes a living parable. The believer who walks by faith is already walking on the border of eternity. One step, and he will simply be home. Faith, for Enoch, was not a doctrine — it was a doorway. He stepped through it and vanished into the presence of the unseen God.

The next portrait is Noah, whose faith built what no one had ever seen.

> *"By faith Noah, being warned of God of things not seen as yet, moved with fear, prepared an ark to the saving of his house; by the which he condemned the world, and became heir of the righteousness which is by faith." (v. 7)*

Noah's faith stands at the intersection of revelation and ridicule. God spoke of judgment that had not yet come—of waters that had not yet fallen. Nothing in Noah's experience or environment supported what he heard. The skies were clear, the world prosperous, and humanity self-assured. Yet the Word of God cut across all appearances, commanding the building of an ark on dry ground.

Faith took that unseen word and made it visible in wood, pitch, and hammer-strokes. For decades Noah worked, his labor a sermon to a watching world. Every beam nailed in place was an act of obedience, every plank a declaration: the unseen Word is true. Noah's faith turned prophecy into architecture—truth into timber.

To the world, his work looked absurd. They saw only a strange old man and his boat. But Noah saw something else: the invisible hand of justice moving toward fulfillment. He moved with fear—not terror of the storm, but reverence for the One who had spoken. True faith takes God seriously. It acts as though His warnings are certain and His promises sure, even when there is no visible evidence of either.

Through obedience, Noah became "heir of the righteousness which is by faith." That phrase is crucial: his righteousness was not earned by the building, but revealed through it. The ark did not make Noah righteous; it made his righteousness visible. His faith manifested an unseen salvation—the same pattern later fulfilled in Christ, whose cross became the ark of our deliverance.

Thus Noah's life testifies that faith does not wait for proof; it becomes proof. It builds in the present what God has declared about the future. It shapes its surroundings according to the unseen. The rains that fell in judgment upon the unbelieving became the same waters that lifted Noah toward safety. In the same way, the very trials that drown unbelief raise the believer who walks by faith.

Noah's hammer still echoes. Every sound of obedience still preaches: the unseen will soon be seen; the eternal word will find its fulfillment. Faith builds before the flood.

The next portrait is Abraham, the father of the faithful, whose entire life was a pilgrimage into the unseen.

"By faith Abraham, when he was called to go out into a place which he should after receive for an inheritance, obeyed; and he went out, not knowing whither he went." (v. 8)

Faith for Abraham began with a call and a command. God spoke, and Abraham obeyed. He left Ur of the Chaldees—a thriving, comfortable city—for a land he had never seen. He traded certainty for promise. That is the pattern of faith: it forsakes what is visible to pursue what is invisible. Faith walks forward on the word of God alone.

Abraham did not move because he understood; he moved because he trusted. The geography of his obedience was uncertain, but the voice that called him was not. Faith does not ask for maps—only for the Word. "He went out, not knowing whither he went." That sentence is the essence of discipleship. The believer who lives by faith walks not by explanation, but by revelation.

"By faith he sojourned in the land of promise, as in a strange country, dwelling in tabernacles with Isaac and Jacob, the heirs with him of the same promise." (v. 9)

Even when Abraham arrived, he never settled. He lived in tents, moving from place to place, always a stranger, always waiting. His faith did not demand possession to believe the promise. He was content to live as a pilgrim because he knew that the promise was not of soil, but of salvation.

"For he looked for a city which hath foundations, whose builder and maker is God." (v. 10)

Here the contrast sharpens. Abraham pitched his tent upon earth, but his heart was anchored in heaven. The cities of men crumble, but the city of God endures. Faith recognizes the difference. It builds temporary shelters in a transient world while fixing its hope upon eternal foundations.

Abraham's journey makes visible the invisible nature of the Christian life. We are heirs of a kingdom we cannot yet see, travelers in a world not our own. Like Abraham, we are called to go out—away from the familiar, away from the security of sight—toward the reality of the promise. His faith carved a path through history for all who would follow after.

The call to Abraham was, in essence, a rehearsal of the gospel. When God said, "Get thee out," it was not merely a command to move, but a call to believe that God's unseen purpose was better than all visible comfort. In leaving Ur, Abraham anticipated Christ, who "left the glory which He had with the Father" to seek and save the lost. In offering Isaac, he foreshadowed Calvary; and in receiving him back, he prefigured resurrection.

Abraham's faith made the invisible visible in every step. He believed the promise when his body was as good as dead, and when Sarah's womb was long barren. Yet he "staggered not at the promise of God through unbelief; but was strong in faith, giving glory to God" (Romans 4:20).

Faith turned his frailty into fruitfulness, his wandering into witness. He saw a city that could not be shaken because he trusted a Word that could not fail. The life of Abraham teaches us that faith does not demand immediate fulfillment—it delights in the unseen certainty of God's character.

When God said, "I will show thee," Abraham stepped into the unknown, and by doing so, made the invisible God visible through obedience.

The next portrait is Sarah, whose faith brought life out of barrenness and laughter out of impossibility.

> *"Through faith also Sarah herself received strength to conceive seed, and was delivered of a child when she was past age, because she judged Him faithful who had promised." (v. 11)*

If Abraham's faith teaches us to walk, Sarah's teaches us to wait. Her story reminds us that faith not only ventures into the unseen but also endures within it. When the promise of a son first came, she laughed. Years of disappointment had dulled hope. The tent of promise had become a place of silence and emptiness. Yet the laughter of disbelief became, in time, the laughter of joy, for God turned her frailty into fruitfulness.

Faith is not the absence of weakness—it is the victory of trust over weakness. The text says she "received strength." She did not summon it from within; it was given. Faith does not depend on human capability but on divine sufficiency. Sarah's faith began not in perfect confidence but in eventual surrender: she judged Him faithful who had promised. That single phrase unlocks the essence of all true faith.

Faith is not believing that we are able; it is believing that He is faithful. It rests not on the probability of fulfillment but on the reliability of the Promiser. Sarah stopped measuring her age and started measuring His faithfulness. The miracle followed.

> *"Therefore sprang there even of one, and him as good as dead, so many as the stars of the sky in multitude, and as the sand which is by the seashore innumerable." (v. 12)*

Out of the impossibility of two aged bodies, God formed a nation. The visible line of Israel became the manifestation of an unseen covenant. Sarah's tent became the cradle of the promise, her laughter the echo of redemption's coming joy.

Here again, faith does not create truth; it cooperates with it. The promise existed before Sarah believed—it was God's decree—but through her faith it entered history. What was invisible became visible through obedience and trust.

Sarah's story speaks to every believer who waits through long years of silence, who struggles with delayed answers and fading strength. God's promises are not hindered by human limitation. He waits until the vessel is empty, so that faith may reveal His fullness. The womb of barrenness became the workshop of grace.

Through Sarah we learn that faith not only moves mountains—it multiplies generations. The same God who brought forth Isaac from the barren brings forth spiritual fruit from believing hearts. When we judge Him faithful, He makes visible what seemed impossible.

Faith Measured in Eternity

"These all died in faith, not having received the promises, but having seen them afar off, and were persuaded of them, and embraced them, and confessed that they were strangers and pilgrims on the earth." (vv. 13–14)

The writer now pauses to gather these lives together beneath one truth: they all died in faith. Each of them obeyed God's Word, lived within His promise, and yet departed this world without ever seeing that promise fully realized. Their eyes closed upon the visible, still fixed on the invisible. Faith accompanied them all the way to their final breath, and beyond.

They "saw" the promises "afar off." Faith gave them sight, not of possession but of perspective. The eyes of faith can see across centuries because they are focused on eternity. They "were persuaded of them, and embraced them." They clung to what they could not yet hold, wrapping their lives around unseen truth.

This is the essence of the pilgrim spirit: to live in tents on earth while owning deeds in heaven. The faithful of old did not mistake their temporary surroundings for their eternal home. They "confessed that they were strangers and pilgrims on the earth." The word confessed implies public declaration — not quiet resignation but open identity. They were unashamed of their homelessness in this world because they had already found their home in another.

> "For they that say such things declare plainly that they seek a country." (v. 14)

The life of faith is a declaration — not only by words, but by how we live. To seek a country is not to wander aimlessly; it is to walk with direction toward a promise unseen. The faithful may appear restless, but their restlessness is holy. Their movement reveals their citizenship.

> "And truly, if they had been mindful of that country from whence they came out, they might have had opportunity to have returned. But now they desire a better country, that is, an heavenly." (vv. 15–16a)

Faith forgets the old homeland. Those who live by faith have burned their bridges to the world behind them. Abraham never longed for Ur again; his tent was pitched toward eternity. Faith leaves the past unrecoverable because it has seen something better ahead. It "desires a better country"—not a better climate or culture, but a heavenly one.

Here the text lifts us from geography to theology. The homeland of faith is not a plot of ground, but a Person. To desire a better country is to desire the presence of God Himself. The faithful hunger for what cannot be shaken because they have glimpsed it in His Word.

"Wherefore God is not ashamed to be called their God: for He hath prepared for them a city."
(v. 16b)

What a statement! The Creator of the universe, who owes no one His approval, publicly identifies Himself with those who live by unseen reality. God is not ashamed of faith. He delights in it, because faith mirrors His own constancy. He prepared for them a city — not a temporary camp or shifting tent, but a permanent dwelling built on divine foundations.

Faith's endurance reveals heaven's affection. The world may call the believer deluded, but God calls him His own. Those who live by faith become living proofs of the invisible kingdom, and when they die, that kingdom opens to receive them.

Faith may begin in obedience and continue in endurance, but it ends in sight. The promises they saw afar off now surround them. The unseen has become their eternal landscape.

Faith Tested and Proven

"By faith Abraham, when he was tried, offered up Isaac: and he that had received the promises offered up his only begotten son, of whom it was said, That in Isaac shall thy seed be called: accounting that God was able to raise him up, even from the dead; from whence also he received him in a figure." (vv. 17–19)

Abraham's journey of faith reaches its highest and hardest point here. The same God who called him out of Ur now calls him to climb a mountain and offer up his promised son. The command struck at everything Abraham believed. Isaac was not merely his child— he was the living embodiment of God's covenant. Every promise God had made was wrapped in that boy's heartbeat.

When God said, "Take now thy son, thine only son Isaac, whom thou lovest," faith faced its most impossible question: Can I trust the God who gives to take away?

Abraham did not understand, but he obeyed. Faith, when mature, does not require explanation; it rests upon God's character. The same voice that once said, "Get thee out," now said, "Offer him up," and Abraham rose early in the morning and went. Faith delayed is weak faith; faith that obeys immediately reveals that the unseen is more real than the visible.

The journey to Moriah must have been agonizing— three days walking beside the son of promise, carrying wood for the altar. Each step was a sermon on surrender. When Isaac asked, "Behold the fire and the wood: but where is the lamb for a burnt offering?" Abraham answered with words that still echo through the ages: "My son, God will provide Himself a lamb."

That sentence holds the heart of redemptive faith. Abraham did not invent comfort for himself; he declared confidence in God's unseen provision. He saw, dimly yet truly, the day of Christ (John 8:56). His faith turned prophetic, announcing what only heaven yet knew: God will provide Himself.

The writer to the Hebrews explains what Abraham reasoned in his heart—he "accounted that God was able to raise him up, even from the dead." The word accounted means he added up the evidence of God's faithfulness and found resurrection the only logical outcome. This was not blind emotion but redeemed reasoning. Faith does not ignore logic; it reorders it around divine truth.

Abraham's hand was stayed, the knife withheld, the substitute provided. Yet in a deeper sense, he still offered Isaac, for in his heart the sacrifice was complete. He yielded his son to the sovereignty of God and received him back "in a figure"—a living picture of resurrection life.

Here the unseen becomes vividly visible. The ram caught in the thicket points to Christ, the true Son whom God did not spare. On that same mountain range centuries later, another Father would offer His only Son, and this time there would be no voice to call from heaven, "Stay thy hand." What Abraham only acted in symbol, God fulfilled in substance.

Faith climbs that mountain still. It lays every treasure on the altar, believing that what is surrendered to God is never lost. Faith does not cling to the gift; it clings to the Giver. And on every hill of obedience, God provides Himself again.

Few realize that Abraham's altar was not built in isolation. The land of Moriah, where God sent him, was not some nameless desert hill but the very ridge upon which Jerusalem would later stand. Scripture connects the two directly:

"Then Solomon began to build the house of the Lord at Jerusalem in Mount Moriah." (2 Chronicles 3:1)

This means Abraham's test took place in the very place where the temple would rise — the same mount where, two thousand years later, the Son of God would be offered. The mountain of Abraham's surrender became the mountain of substitution.

The scene we often picture in solitude was, in all likelihood, set within sight of the city's inhabitants. Abraham was known there already, for Genesis 14 tells us he had met Melchizedek, king of Salem, centuries before it was called Jerusalem. What God commanded, then, was not a private act of devotion but a public declaration. The friend of God ascended the hill of the future temple and enacted, before human eyes, the drama of redemption that would define history.

If Abraham had faltered, the surrounding nations would have seen only a confused old man and a silent God. Instead, they witnessed a substitute caught in the thicket — the visible evidence of God's mercy. Faith's obedience turned theology into spectacle.

So too with us. God often calls His children to endure tests not in secret, but in full view of the watching world. We would rather wrestle alone in the wilderness, but He places us where faith can be seen. The struggle becomes a testimony; the surrender becomes a sermon. When we obey on the public stage of trial, others see the ram in the thicket — the provision of God revealed through our faith.

Faith Looking Forward

"By faith Isaac blessed Jacob and Esau concerning things to come.

By faith Jacob, when he was dying, blessed both the sons of Joseph; and worshiped, leaning upon the top of his staff.

By faith Joseph, when he died, made mention of the departing of the children of Israel; and gave commandment concerning his bones." (vv. 20–22)

The narrative slows here. We move from the mountains of testing to the deathbeds of faith. The spotlight shifts from action to anticipation. No altars are built, no seas parted, no enemies conquered — only quiet words spoken over sons and futures. Yet these verses reveal faith's endurance more than any miracle could. The patriarchs are dying, but they are still believing.

Isaac blessed his sons "concerning things to come." His physical eyes were dim, yet the eyes of faith still saw the line of promise stretching beyond his lifetime. Though he mistakenly blessed Jacob thinking him Esau, God's purpose stood. Faith may stumble in execution, but it stands in direction — it believes forward.

Jacob, leaning on his staff, blessed both the sons of Joseph. The scene is intimate: an old man worshiping at the end of his days, his body frail but his vision strong. Faith does not end when strength fails; it often shines brightest then. Jacob's bent frame and lifted heart picture the paradox of faith — weakness carrying worship, mortality embracing eternity. He saw in Ephraim and Manasseh not just grandsons but nations — visible heirs of an invisible covenant.

Joseph, the final patriarch in this sequence, believed through four centuries of silence. As he lay dying in Egypt, he made his family swear to carry his bones back to Canaan when God fulfilled His word. "God will surely visit you," he said (Genesis 50:25). That phrase is pure faith — a declaration spoken into generations unborn. Joseph looked across time and saw deliverance before it came. His unburied bones became a prophecy in waiting, a silent sermon through the years of bondage: God will visit you.

Together these three testimonies remind us that faith outlives the flesh. It speaks when the voice is gone, prays when the pulse is faint, blesses when the breath is short. True faith does not expire at death; it looks through death to resurrection. Isaac, Jacob, and Joseph all died with unfinished stories, yet they died holding the unshakable Word. They made visible, in their dying, the reality that God's promises cannot die.

Faith begins by obeying God's Word, grows by enduring delay, and culminates in the ability to die in peace. The patriarchs show that faith's last breath is often its clearest testimony.

Faith Choosing Reproach Over Reward

"By faith Moses, when he was born, was hid three months of his parents, because they saw he was a proper child; and they were not afraid of the king's commandment.

By faith Moses, when he was come to years, refused to be called the son of Pharaoh's daughter; choosing rather to suffer affliction with the people of God, than to enjoy the pleasures of sin for a season; esteeming the reproach of Christ greater riches than the treasures in Egypt: for he had respect unto the recompense of the reward." (vv. 23–26)

Faith's story now moves from the quiet trust of patriarchs to the defiant courage of deliverance. Moses' life begins in the cradle of danger and ends in the camp of redemption, and both ends of that life are framed by faith.

First, faith saw something. His parents saw that he was "a proper child" — not merely beautiful in appearance, but marked by divine purpose. They hid him, not out of sentiment, but out of confidence that God's plan overruled Pharaoh's decree. Faith does not fear the wrath of kings when it sees the sovereignty of God. The same faith that sustained those parents in secrecy would later sustain their son in confrontation.

When Moses "was come to years," faith chose. He had every visible reason to remain in Egypt — wealth, education, security, and power — yet he turned away from all of it. He "refused to be called the son of Pharaoh's daughter." That word refused is strong; it means he deliberately rejected the identity the world offered him. Faith does not accept temporary comfort when it obscures eternal calling.

He "chose rather to suffer affliction with the people of God, than to enjoy the pleasures of sin for a season." The pleasures of Egypt were real, but they were seasonal. Faith sees the expiration date stamped upon worldly reward. Moses valued reproach over riches because faith measures wealth by eternity. He looked past Pharaoh's palace and saw Christ's glory. The text says he "esteemed the reproach of Christ greater riches." That phrase bridges the covenants — showing that even in Moses' day, faith was Christ-centered. The suffering of God's people in Egypt was, in seed form, the suffering of Christ for His people on the cross.

Faith always values the invisible more than the visible, and therefore chooses differently. To the world, Moses' choice looked foolish; to heaven, it looked faithful.

"By faith he forsook Egypt, not fearing the wrath of the king: for he endured, as seeing Him who is invisible." (v. 27)

That verse distills Moses' secret. He endured as seeing Him who is invisible. Faith's sight is not mystical but moral — a clear perception of unseen truth. Moses endured not because he was fearless, but because he saw God more vividly than he saw Pharaoh. When the invisible becomes more real than the visible, endurance becomes natural.

"Through faith he kept the Passover, and the sprinkling of blood, lest he that destroyed the firstborn should touch them." (v. 28)

Faith not only renounces the world's riches; it receives God's redemption. The same man who once struck the Egyptian in anger now obeys precisely, applying blood to doorposts as God commanded. Faith learns to fight no longer with sword or status, but with obedience. The blood upon the lintel was invisible protection made visible — faith's testimony painted in crimson.

"By faith they passed through the Red Sea as by dry land: which the Egyptians assaying to do were drowned." (v. 29)

Here faith moves from the individual to the corporate. The people followed Moses through the parted waters, each step a defiance of logic. The sea's walls towered over them, but faith saw a pathway, not a trap. Egypt's armies saw the same corridor but entered without faith — and perished. The difference between deliverance and destruction was not visibility but belief. The same sea that judged Egypt saved Israel, just as the same cross that condemns unbelief redeems faith.

Moses' story shows that faith not only obeys in private but resists in public. It refuses the crown of comfort to bear the cross of reproach. It leaves palaces behind to follow the unseen King. Faith endures, as seeing Him who is invisible — and in doing so, makes that invisible King known.

Faith Obeying and Waiting

"By faith the walls of Jericho fell down, after they were compassed about seven days. By faith the harlot Rahab perished not with them that believed not, when she had received the spies with peace." (vv. 30–31)

The conquest of Jericho reveals faith's strength in both action and patience. Israel's faith was not proven by warfare but by obedience — marching in circles around a city while the world watched in scorn. Faith often appears foolish before it is vindicated. For six days, the people walked without speaking, trusting that silent obedience would achieve what strategy never could. Every step declared that the battle belonged to the Lord, not to their weapons.

And yet within those same walls, faith took another form. While Israel's faith marched, Rahab's faith waited. She had received the spies in peace, believed the word they brought, and tied the scarlet cord in her window — the visible mark of invisible grace.

Faith Waiting Under the Scarlet Sign

"And the second day they marched around the city once and returned to the camp. So they did six days." (Joshua 6:14)

Picture Rahab and her household through those long days of delay. They had heard of God's power — how He stopped the Jordan's floodwaters and brought His people to the very gates of Jericho. The city was trembling, yet deliverance did not come. Each day began with the sound of distant trumpets, grew to the thunder of marching feet, and ended in silence. The army of God came and went, and the city still stood.

For six days, Rahab's family waited beneath that crimson cord. They knew nothing of God's battle plan — only His promise. They could not predict the timing, only trust the Word. Waiting became their warfare.

Can we not feel their tension? Each night they must have wondered, Has the promise failed? Each morning they chose to stay put, clinging to the sign of grace while the city around them mocked their hope. Faith was tested not by pain, but by patience.

But on the seventh day, everything changed. The march did not end; the sound did not fade. The trumpets continued, the shouting rose, and the walls began to crumble. The house under the scarlet cord stood firm. The family that waited in faith walked out in victory.

Rahab's story is not only about deliverance — it is about enduring expectation. The God who redeemed her did so not instantly, but in time. Her faith held when all visible evidence said to despair.

The church stands in a similar place today. Like Rahab's household, we live inside a city destined for judgment but marked by grace. The scarlet sign is above us — the blood of the Lamb. We know the armies of heaven are near; we can almost hear the trumpets tuning. Yet we are called to wait. The walls still stand, the world still mocks, but the promise remains sure.

Faith under the scarlet sign does not wander, doubt, or blend in. It stays near the window of redemption. It waits where grace has placed it. And when the final trumpet sounds, every soul sheltered beneath the blood will stand.

Faith marches when commanded and waits when told. In both, it manifests unseen reality. The unseen Deliverer is coming; until then, the scarlet cord still holds.

Faith Unconquered

"And what shall I more say? for the time would fail me to tell of Gideon, and of Barak, and of Samson, and of Jephthah; of David also, and Samuel, and of the prophets: who through faith subdued kingdoms, wrought righteousness, obtained promises, stopped the mouths of lions, quenched the violence of fire, escaped the edge of the sword, out of weakness were made strong, waxed valiant in fight, turned to flight the armies of the aliens." (vv. 32–34)

The writer's tone quickens now. The names come like the rush of a river, each one another stone in faith's foundation. The time would fail to recount them all — and indeed, history could not contain the fullness of faith's triumphs. Through faith, kingdoms fell and righteousness flourished. Lions' mouths were closed, flames quenched, swords blunted, and the weak made mighty. Faith is the unseen power behind every visible victory.

"Women received their dead raised to life again: and others were tortured, not accepting deliverance; that they might obtain a better resurrection." (v. 35)

Here the text turns — victory and suffering stand side by side, equally crowned with faith. Those who saw deliverance and those who endured death belong to the same company. Faith's greatness is not measured by outcome but by obedience. Some triumphed, others perished — both believed. Some were delivered from fire; others met God in the midst of it. Both bore witness to the same unseen reality: that God is faithful whether He rescues or receives.

> *"And others had trial of cruel mockings and scourgings, yea, moreover of bonds and imprisonment: they were stoned, they were sawn asunder, were tempted, were slain with the sword: they wandered about in sheepskins and goatskins; being destitute, afflicted, tormented; (of whom the world was not worthy:) they wandered in deserts, and in mountains, and in dens and caves of the earth." (vv. 36–38)*

The pace slows again, not in weakness but in awe. The gallery of faith ends not in palaces but in caves. Faith's heroes are destitute in the eyes of men yet priceless in the eyes of God. "Of whom the world was not worthy." That phrase could hang over every generation of saints who have suffered for righteousness. The world calls them fools; heaven calls them faithful. They did not fit because they belonged elsewhere — citizens of an unshakable kingdom still unseen.

> *"And these all, having obtained a good report through faith, received not the promise: God having provided some better thing for us, that they without us should not be made perfect."* (vv. 39–40)

The chapter ends as it began — with unseen fulfillment. All these lived and died by faith, and yet "received not the promise." The promise awaited a fuller revelation: Christ Himself, the fulfillment of every shadow and sacrifice. Their faith looked forward to what ours looks back upon. The cross is the hinge that joins their waiting to our witnessing.

And yet even now, the story is not finished. God has "provided some better thing for us" — the final perfection that awaits all His people together. The saints of the past and the church of the present will be completed as one body when faith gives way to sight. The unseen kingdom they longed for and we proclaim will finally appear in glory.

Faith, then, is not a relic of the past but the lifeblood of the redeemed. It conquers, it endures, it waits, and it suffers — always acting upon the unseen word of God. The world may call such faith madness, but heaven calls it maturity.

The eleventh chapter of Hebrews is not a museum of heroes; it is a mirror held before the church. The same unseen King who ruled their hearts rules ours still. The same faith that framed their obedience must form ours. The world is still watching, and the walls have not yet fallen — but they will. Until that day, we walk, wait, and worship by faith, "as seeing Him who is invisible."

Application — Faith's Present Challenge

We, too, are called to make the invisible visible. Faith is not verified by what we feel but by what we do. Anyone can say, "I believe"; the question is whether that belief becomes substance—something tangible in our behavior.

James wrote, "Show me thy faith without thy works, and I will show thee my faith by my works." Faith without obedience is invisible. Faith with obedience becomes evidence.

Perhaps you wrestle with doubt. Perhaps you cannot yet say that you understand how God is working. Then live as though you do. Pray, read, serve, obey— act on the truth you know, and God will reveal more. Faith is exercised into strength. You cannot feel your way into faith; you must act your way into sight.

Conclusion — Faith and the Eternal Kingdom

The visible world is temporary. Every monument of human pride decays. Drive down a country road and you'll see the remains of someone's dream home— roof caved in, porch falling off, the memory of laughter replaced by silence. Once it was precious. Now it is forgotten.

That is what life looks like when it is built only for the visible.

But the life built on unseen truth never collapses. Those who live by faith are already citizens of an unshakable kingdom. Their obedience participates in eternity. As Jesus said, "Lay up for yourselves treasures in heaven."

Without faith, nothing you do will last.

But with faith, all things are possible.

Faith is not wishing—it is working.

Faith is not feeling—it is following.

Faith brings the invisible God into visible reality through obedient action.

Prayer

Father,

We thank You for the witness of those who lived by faith before us—who walked, obeyed, and suffered, believing what they could not yet see. Teach us to live by the same substance of truth. Deliver us from the shallow comfort of feelings and give us courage for faithful action. May our obedience make Your unseen kingdom visible in this world, and may our lives testify to realities that cannot be shaken.

In Jesus' name, Amen.

7

Run the Race with Endurance: The Father's Discipline (Hebrews 12:1–17)

Faith is not a feeling—it is motion. It is not verified by what we say we believe but by what we live as true. The writer of Hebrews pictures the Christian life as a long-distance race: strenuous, demanding, but joyful.

> *"Wherefore seeing we also are compassed about with so great a cloud of witnesses, let us lay aside every weight, and the sin which doth so easily beset us, and let us run with patience the race that is set before us, Looking unto Jesus the author and finisher of our faith; who for the joy that was set before him endured the cross, despising the shame, and is set down at*

the right hand of the throne of God." (Hebrews 12:1–2)

That word "*compassed*" means surrounded, encircled. The picture is not of distant onlookers in stadium seats, but of veterans crowding the track, cheering on new runners. They are not spectators but witnesses—testifiers—that God is faithful and that the race can be finished. Their lives, recorded in Scripture, stand as evidence that ordinary people can endure by extraordinary grace.

Clearing the Lane

The Spirit's command is clear: *"Let us lay aside every weight, and the sin which doth so easily beset us."* Every serious runner knows that what you carry determines how far you can go. In the Greek games, runners would strip away everything unnecessary—every strap, every fold, every ounce of drag—because the smallest resistance could mean the difference between victory and collapse.

The word translated "*weight*" can also describe a swelling or growth. The ancient Greeks even used it medically to refer to a tumor. The image is vivid: some burdens are not moral but physical, emotional, or habitual. They are things that grow quietly in our lives until they begin to weigh us down. They are not sin in themselves, but they feed sin. They slow obedience. They distract affection. They divide attention.

You might not even notice when the weight forms. A habit of comparison, an obsession with approval, an addiction to convenience—all these can add bulk to the soul. The writer doesn't tell us to pray about our weights or analyze them; he says to lay them aside. Runners don't reason with weights—they drop them.

Then he adds, *"and the sin which doth so easily beset us."* The phrase literally means "the sin that wraps around the feet." It is the picture of a runner tangled in vines—trying to move, but tripped by what clings close. Everyone has a sin that fits easily, a sin that feels natural. For some it is anger; for others, pride, lust, or fear. Whatever it is, it must be put off daily, deliberately, decisively.

The Race Set Before Us

The Christian life is not a sprint but a marathon. It is not about speed but stamina—not about bursts of enthusiasm but about steady endurance. The race is "set before us," meaning appointed by God. You do not choose your track; God does. He marks the course, sets the pace, and determines the finish line.

The call is to run "with patience." The word here— ὑπομονή (*hupomonē*)—is one of the richest in the

New Testament. It means to remain under, to stay steadfast beneath pressure. It is not passive resignation but active endurance—the strength that holds steady while weight bears down.

The Arch of Faith

The ancients knew something about strength under pressure. In the first century, the architectural symbol of permanence was the arch. At first glance, an arch should collapse. It has no center support—only stones leaning inward against each other. Yet the more weight that presses down on it, the stronger it becomes. Why? Because the downward force drives the stones together. At the center sits the keystone, the single wedge that distributes pressure and binds every other stone in place.

That is the picture of the church—and of faith itself. Christ is our Keystone. Each believer is a stone set into His design. When the pressures of life bear down, when the weight of sorrow, loss, and conflict seems unbearable, the Keystone holds—and the pressure actually strengthens the whole. Without weight, the arch falls apart. With weight rightly distributed through Christ, it stands forever.

So when the writer says, "Run with patience," he means: stay under the weight; don't quit the arch. Let the pressure drive you closer to Christ and to one another. Faith does not remove pressure; it redeems it.

Looking Unto Jesus

The direction of faith matters as much as its endurance. "Looking unto Jesus, the author and finisher of our faith." Faith is not a blind leap but a fixed gaze. The word means to "look away from all else." We cannot look at our wounds, our rivals, or our surroundings; our eyes must be locked on the Captain who ran ahead.

The writer calls Him both Author and Finisher. In Hebrews 2:10, the same Greek word is translated Captain—ἀρχηγός (archēgos), meaning pioneer, leader, founder. It was a word used for the leader of a new colony. When a city in Greece wanted to plant a colony abroad, they sent an archēgos ahead to prepare the land, lay foundations, and establish order. Only when the place was ready would he return for the citizens and lead them to the new home.

That is who Jesus is for us—the Captain of our salvation, the Pioneer of a new world. He has gone before to prepare a place for us (John 14:2), and now He runs beside us, urging us toward the finish line He Himself has crossed.

But He is also the Finisher—τελειωτής (*teleiōtēs*), the One who perfects. He doesn't merely start faith; He completes it. He doesn't just write the opening line; He finishes the story.

Why does this matter? Because there are seasons when you start running in joy and finish in tears. There are days when your faith wavers, when you trip, when your pace falters. Yet the Finisher never falters. He picks up what you drop. He completes what you begin.

Enduring the Cross

The passage continues:

"Who for the joy that was set before Him endured the cross, despising the shame, and is set down at the right hand of the throne of God."

Endurance is not stoicism. It is joy that looks through pain to promise. Christ endured the cross not because He enjoyed suffering, but because He loved the outcome. The joy "set before Him" was the joy of redemption—the joy of reconciling us to the Father, the joy of seeing sinners forgiven and heaven opened to humanity.

He despised the shame. That word "despised" means He counted it as nothing in comparison to what lay ahead. The ridicule, the humiliation, the agony—all real, all terrible—but temporary. He endured it for eternal joy.

When we set our eyes on Him, endurance becomes possible. We see in His suffering the model and the meaning of ours. The cross was not the defeat of faith but its demonstration.

Hebrews 12:3–17 — The Father's Discipline and Our Endurance

"For consider him that endured such contradiction of sinners against himself, lest ye be wearied and faint in your minds. Ye have not yet resisted unto blood, striving against sin. And ye have forgotten the exhortation which speaketh unto you as unto children, My son, despise not thou the chastening of the Lord, nor faint when thou art rebuked of him: For whom the Lord loveth he chasteneth, and scourgeth every son whom he receiveth." (Heb. 12:3–6)

The Example That Steadies the Heart

The first medicine for weariness is not rest but remembrance. "Consider him."

When discouragement starts whispering that obedience is not worth it, the writer does not tell us to look within but to look to Jesus. He endured contradiction—open resistance from sinners, slander from the righteous, betrayal from friends, and the cross from His enemies. He kept running when every voice told Him to stop. Why? Because He had already fixed His eyes on the joy beyond the shame.

The Hebrew believers had known ridicule, property loss, even imprisonment (Heb. 10:32–34), but most had not yet bled for their faith. The writer reminds them—and us—that if Christ endured, we can endure. Our race is hard; His was harder. Our pain is temporary; His won eternity.

Faith strengthens when it remembers the pattern of the Captain.

The Forgotten Exhortation

"And ye have forgotten the exhortation which speaketh unto you as unto children..."

Faith fatigue often comes from spiritual amnesia. We forget what God already told us. Here the author quotes Proverbs 3:11-12, reminding believers that discipline is not rejection—it is relationship. The Father's correction is proof of sonship.

Human instinct misreads pain: we assume trouble means God is displeased. But in the economy of grace, discipline is not retribution but refinement. Punishment looks backward to guilt; chastening looks forward to glory. The Father never punishes the believer, because all punishment fell on the Son. At Calvary, the gavel of divine justice struck once, and the case was closed. What remains is the patient correction of a loving Parent who refuses to leave His children weak or wild.

Punishment vs. Chastening

Punishment	Chastening
Flowing from wrath	Flowing from love
Aims to condemn	Aims to correct
Looks backward (to sin committed)	Looks forward (to holiness desired)
Administered by a judge	Administered by a father
Ends in separation	Ends in restoration

Christ took our punishment once for all (Isa. 53:5; Rom. 8:1). The Father now gives chastening so that we might "be partakers of His holiness." The difference changes everything. When hardship comes, the believer no longer cries, "God must be angry with me!" but "God must be shaping me!" One response leads to despair; the other, to worship.

The Trainer's Wisdom

Verse 11 captures the process perfectly: *"Now no chastening for the present seemeth to be joyous, but grievous: nevertheless afterward it yieldeth the peaceable fruit of righteousness unto them which are exercised thereby."*

The word "exercised" is athletic—it means to be trained through repetition until strength becomes habit. Discipline is not random pain; it is a training program. The Father is a master coach who knows when to stretch us, when to rest us, and when to press us past what we thought possible.

A Christian who refuses discipline forfeits development. The believer who welcomes it grows spiritual muscle. The same weight that crushes one will strengthen another depending on how they yield beneath it.

Every serious runner knows this principle: fatigue builds endurance. When muscles tear under stress, they heal stronger. So does faith. God's chastening is never punitive pain—it is constructive pressure.

Think of an apprentice learning under a craftsman. The master corrects his hand, sometimes sharply, not because he dislikes the student, but because he wants the work to be beautiful. The blows of the chisel are part of the sculpture.

Hands That Hang Down

"Wherefore lift up the hands which hang down, and the feeble knees." (v. 12)

Discipline is never meant to leave us collapsed in the dust. God's correction strengthens what it strikes. The hands droop when faith falters; knees wobble when hope wanes. The call is not merely individual— it is corporate. When you see a brother sagging under the strain, lift his arms. When you see a sister's knees buckling, come alongside.

Running is easier with companions. The Christian race is not a solo marathon but a relay of grace. Every church is a training field where tired saints learn to stand again.

Make Straight Paths

"And make straight paths for your feet, lest that which is lame be turned out of the way; but let it rather be healed." (v. 13)

The picture is of a rough trail full of ruts and rocks. An injured runner needs a smooth lane, not an obstacle course. The mature believer clears the road for the weak. We remove stumbling blocks, not scatter them.

A church that gossips, quarrels, or tolerates bitterness becomes a dangerous track. The lame stumble there. But a church that practices grace—clear, honest, humble grace—becomes a healing lane where the wounded can run again.

Follow Peace and Holiness

"Follow peace with all men, and holiness, without which no man shall see the Lord." (v. 14)

Two pursuits define maturity: peace and holiness. Peace is relational holiness; holiness is moral peace. To follow them is to chase them down—to make them priorities worth effort.

Peace is not the absence of conflict but the presence of reconciliation. Holiness is not the absence of error but the presence of Christlikeness. The two always travel together. A peaceful heart without holiness is compromise; holiness without peace is pride. Only their union reveals the Lord to the watching world.

When believers choose forgiveness over retaliation, they make the invisible God visible. When they choose purity over applause, they display His nature. That is how the church "sees the Lord"—not by mystical vision but by moral resemblance.

The Root of Bitterness

"Looking diligently lest any man fail of the grace of God; lest any root of bitterness springing up trouble you, and thereby many be defiled." (v. 15)

Bitterness is a weed with underground ambition. It hides until it owns the field. One offense, one grudge left unconfessed, becomes a root system that chokes grace. The warning is corporate—"many be defiled." Bitterness spreads faster than faith.

A wise farmer once told me that before planting season he would "burn the rows." He'd drag a small flame torch across the field to kill unseen weed seed before the crop went in. That is what confession and forgiveness do in the soul—they burn the field before fruit appears. Unforgiven hurts are dormant weeds waiting for spring. The fire of repentance keeps the soil clear for grace to grow.

Esau's Exchange

"Lest there be any fornicator, or profane person, as Esau, who for one morsel of meat sold his birthright." (v. 16)

Esau is the tragic end of unchecked appetite. He sold eternal inheritance for a single meal. The writer calls him profane—not because he cursed, but because he treated holy things as common. That is the essence of profanity: to take what God calls sacred and treat it as ordinary.

Every temptation whispers, "It's just one bite." Every compromise says, "You can always get it back later." But Esau's story warns us: some losses cannot be undone. Once he ate, the bowl was empty and the birthright gone. Tears could not reverse it.

When faith forgets its future, it will sell its soul for the present. But when faith looks to the eternal, it will wait for the feast to come.

The Fruit of Discipline

"Nevertheless afterward it yieldeth the peaceable fruit of righteousness unto them which are exercised thereby." (v. 11)

That is the promise hanging over every hardship. God's discipline yields fruit—peaceable, righteous, lasting. The storms that bend the tree also deepen its roots. The weight that tires the runner also tones his strength. The Father wastes no pain. Every strike of His hand is measured, and every blow of His chisel is aimed at beauty.

The result of discipline is not despair but maturity—a quiet, resilient righteousness that neither boasts nor breaks. The church needs such saints: not those who never limp, but those who limp toward glory with joy.

Endurance Together

The whole passage moves from the individual to the communal—from "run your race" to "help others run theirs." The Father's discipline is personal, but its fruit is public. A disciplined church becomes a gracious church—a community that corrects without cruelty, forgives without delay, and endures without division.

Every time we endure together, we remind the world that Christ is enough. Every act of patience, every shared burden, every reconciled relationship becomes a testimony that we are sons and daughters, not strangers and slaves.

The same God who trains us under pressure also unites us under grace. The same fire that burns away our pride refines our fellowship. The same Father who disciplines individuals builds a family that endures forever.

Summary

Faith runs long. We cut weights and sins; we look to Jesus, the Captain and Completer; we accept the Father's loving chastening—not wrath, but training—so that we share His holiness. We run together, guarding peace and holiness, uprooting bitterness, and preferring birthright to bowl.

Application

- **Name your weights.** List the good things that have become heavy things. What "tumors" must be cut to run?

- **Submit to the program.** Receive the season you are in as training, not as accident. Ask: What holiness is this trial building?

- **Fix your gaze.** Set a daily "look unto Jesus" habit —Scripture first, prayer first—before news, tasks, or noise.

- **Uproot bitterness early.** Confess grievances before they root. Seek peace quickly; forgive as forgiven.

- **Pace someone.** Put your arm around a weary runner this week—pray with them, walk with them, lighten their load.

- **Despise the stew.** Identify the "one morsel" that tempts you to trade away your birthright, and starve it.

Prayer

Father,
we thank You for love that disciplines, not
wrath that condemns. Train us to run light—
free of weights, clean of entangling sin. Grow
in us the peaceable fruit of righteousness.
Make us a people who lift the weak,
straighten paths, and pursue holiness
together. Guard us from bitterness; teach us
to value our birthright above every morsel.
Strengthen our hands and knees for the race
set before us.
In Jesus' name, Amen.

8

A Kingdom That Cannot Be Moved (Hebrews 12:18–29)

The race of faith does not end in exhaustion but in arrival. The runner lifts his eyes and sees where the course leads—not to the trembling slopes of Sinai but to the living city of Zion. The Christian's goal is not escape from the world but entrance into a kingdom that cannot be shaken.

> *"For ye are not come unto the mount that might be touched, and that burned with fire, nor unto blackness, and darkness, and tempest..."* (Heb. 12:18)

From Sinai to Zion

The author of Hebrews paints a contrast so sharp that the reader can almost hear thunder echoing behind it.

"Ye are not come unto the mount that might be touched, and that burned with fire..." (Heb. 12:18). The two mountains—Sinai and Zion—are more than geography; they are two ways of approaching God, two covenants, two worlds.

At Sinai, Israel stood at the base of a mountain that smoked with divine presence. Exodus 19 tells us that the Lord descended upon it in fire, the whole mount quaking greatly. Lightning tore the sky, trumpets blared, and the people begged that no further word be spoken to them. Even Moses, who had walked into the cloud, said, "I exceedingly fear and quake." The lesson was unmistakable: holiness is unapproachable without mediation. Sinai revealed the distance between man and God.

Everything about that scene said, "Stay back." The boundary ropes, the thunder, the forbidden touch— each shouted the same truth: the sinner cannot draw near. The law was holy, but it could not make its hearers holy. It exposed guilt, but offered no cure. At Sinai, Israel learned reverence, but not yet reconciliation.

Then, across the centuries, the writer of Hebrews points us to another mountain—to Zion, the city of the living God. Here, the tone changes entirely. Where Sinai burned with fire, Zion glows with glory. Where Sinai thundered warnings, Zion sings welcome. Sinai's law carved condemnation into stone; Zion's gospel writes mercy on hearts of flesh. Sinai was the mountain of command; Zion is the mountain of communion.

At Sinai, only Moses ascended; at Zion, "ye are come." The invitation is plural, communal, inclusive. The redeemed are not spectators watching a mediator ascend—they are citizens of the city of God, ascending by faith with their Mediator.

Sinai's fire terrified; Zion's fire transforms. Sinai said, "Do this and live." Zion declares, "It is finished." Sinai showed what righteousness demanded; Zion reveals what righteousness supplied.

The trembling Israelites at Sinai represent all humanity—awed, condemned, and distant. But the rejoicing saints at Zion represent the church—pardoned, adopted, and at home. The same God speaks from both mountains, but through different covenants. At Sinai, He spoke through thunder; at Zion, through the blood of His Son. Holiness has not changed, but access has.

Out of the Iron Furnace

When Moses described Israel's deliverance from Egypt, he chose an image that burned itself into the nation's collective memory:

211

"The LORD hath taken you, and brought you forth out of the iron furnace, even out of Egypt, to be unto him a people of inheritance" (Deut. 4:20).

To the ancient world, iron was not common metal—it was a wonder. Egypt had bronze by the ton, but iron by the ounce. Ordinary furnaces could not reach the temperatures needed to smelt iron ore; the metal remained locked in rock, impossible for men to mine in large quantity. What little iron they possessed fell from the heavens—meteorites streaking through the night sky and embedding themselves in the sand. Priests called it "the metal of heaven." It was rare, sacred, and reserved for the Pharaoh and his nobles. Bronze armed soldiers; iron armed kings.

And God took that image and preached through it: *"I brought you out of the iron furnace."* He was saying, "You were My fallen metal—celestial material buried in bondage. I drew you out, refined you, and reserved you for Myself." As Egypt reserved its iron for royalty, God reserved Israel for His glory. The nobility of Egypt claimed heaven's metal; the holiness of God claimed heaven's people.

The "iron furnace" was both affliction and consecration. Egypt's bondage was real, but so was its purpose. The fire of slavery became the forge of sanctification. They entered the furnace as a mass of slaves; they emerged as a nation of priests. The pressure purified their identity. They were not being discarded—they were being shaped.

The same is true for the believer. Trials are not random heat but refining fire. God wastes no suffering. He uses pain as the crucible of holiness. What feels like destruction is often construction in disguise. The hammer that strikes is the same hand that shapes.

When God descended in fire at Sinai, it was the same flame seen in the furnace of Egypt—holy fire, not to destroy, but to reveal. The mountain's blaze showed them that approach to a holy God without a mediator is impossible. The furnace taught endurance; the mountain taught reverence. Both prepared them for another hill yet to come—Calvary—where the fire of judgment would fall once more, this time on the Lamb.

At the cross, the Son of God entered the furnace. Divine wrath burned against sin, and He bore it willingly. The flames that would have consumed us were absorbed by Him. The fire fell on the Substitute so that it could spare the sinner.

Now, every believer stands as a vessel drawn from the furnace—refined, claimed, and fitted for the Master's use. Sanctification is the slow cooling of molten faith into steadfast form. What began in suffering ends in strength. The God who refines His people never abandons the forge until the reflection of His own face shines back from the metal.

The Israelites could not yet see it, but their story in Egypt was the first spark of the gospel. The world's impossible metal had become God's chosen symbol: heaven's material, purified on earth, reserved for eternity. The iron furnace was never about punishment—it was about purpose. And the God who brought them out of it still forges worshipers from fire.

The Mediator of the New Covenant

Between Sinai and Zion stands a hill called Calvary. The writer of Hebrews directs our gaze there when he says,

> *"Ye are come... to Jesus the mediator of the New Covenant, and to the blood of sprinkling, that speaketh better things than that of Abel"* (Heb. 12:24).

At Sinai, God's holiness and man's sin met face to face—and there was no mediator strong enough to stand between them. Moses climbed the mountain trembling, and even he said, "I exceedingly fear and quake." He could bring the law down to the people, but he could not lift the people up to God. The law could diagnose sin but not cure it. It could point out guilt but not remove it. The thunder was true, but it offered no shelter.

But where the first mediator trembled, the second triumphed. Christ ascended not Mount Sinai but Mount Calvary—alone, carrying not tablets of stone but a cross of wood. And when He reached the summit, He did not say, "Stay back." He stretched out His arms and cried, "Come unto Me."

The Meaning of Mediator

The Greek word *mesitēs* means more than a go-between—it means the medium itself, the channel through which two realities meet. In Him, heaven and earth do not merely shake hands; they share substance. The Son is not simply a negotiator pleading for compromise. He is the medium of reconciliation itself—the living bridge where God's holiness and human sinfulness converge in one Person.

In the Old Covenant, the priest stood beside the altar, sprinkling blood that symbolized atonement. In the new, the Priest is the altar, the offering, and the blood. At Sinai, the mediator offered sacrifices for others. At Calvary, the Mediator was the sacrifice for all.

Moses brought commandments written by the finger of God; Christ bore the wounds of those commandments in His hands. Moses heard the voice from the fire; Christ was the Word made flesh. Moses veiled his face before glory; Christ unveiled the glory of God in human form. The old mediator carried fear; the new Mediator carries fellowship.

The Blood That Speaks Better Things

Abel's blood cried from the ground, demanding justice. It was the voice of injury, the plea of a wronged brother. "The voice of thy brother's blood crieth unto Me from the ground," God said in Genesis 4. Abel's blood called for vengeance; Christ's blood calls for vindication through mercy. Abel's blood demanded retribution; Christ's blood delivers reconciliation. The one cried, "Guilty!"; the other cries, "Forgiven!"

Every drop that fell from His brow, His hands, and His side became a word in heaven's courtroom—words stronger than condemnation, words that never fade. The blood of Christ does not dry or fade; it continues to speak, to intercede, to answer every accusation.

In the Old Covenant, the priest's sacrifice was offered and forgotten, its power spent by sundown. But the blood of Christ does not expire. It lives. It speaks still. It speaks better things—not louder, but deeper. It is not the shout of vengeance, but the song of victory.

The believer does not stand at Sinai, listening to thunder and trembling at law; he stands at Zion, listening to the voice of blood speaking peace. In that voice, fear falls silent. The trembling soul hears a new commandment, written not on stone but on spirit: "Be still, and know that I am God."

The "blood of sprinkling" recalls the old Passover night, when Israel marked their doors with lamb's blood and judgment passed over. That ancient pattern was a shadow; Calvary is the substance. Now, through the blood of the true Lamb, judgment has passed over forever. Death has seen the mark and moved on. The cry of justice has been answered by grace.

This is the heart of Zion's joy—the God who once thundered from fire now speaks through blood. His holiness has not diminished, but His approach has changed. The covenant has shifted from fear to fellowship, from trembling to trust. The Mediator stands eternal, bearing the marks that bought our peace.

And now the Christian life is lived not beneath a mountain of smoke, but beneath a cross of mercy. The same voice still speaks, but not in judgment; it speaks in intercession. He who mediated once on Calvary now mediates forever in glory. The covenant cannot be revoked because the blood cannot be removed.

The Voice That Shakes the Earth

The writer now returns to the image of God's voice—thundering once from Sinai, now echoing through the gospel.

> *"See that ye refuse not him that speaketh. For if they escaped not who refused him that spake on earth, much more shall not we escape, if we turn away from him that speaketh from heaven: whose voice then shook the earth: but now he hath promised, saying, Yet once more I shake not the earth only, but also heaven." (Heb. 12:25-26)*

At Sinai, the ground itself trembled beneath Israel's feet. Dust rose in waves, stones split, and even creation seemed to recoil before the majesty of its Maker. But that shaking was local—a small foretaste of a greater disturbance still to come. The prophet Haggai foresaw it centuries later: "Yet once more, in a little while, I will shake the heavens and the earth, the sea and the dry land; and I will fill this house with glory." (Hag. 2:6-7). That prophecy began its fulfillment when Christ entered the world. The Incarnation itself was the first tremor—God's Word made flesh breaking into history's crust.

Every time God speaks, something shakes. His voice never leaves creation unchanged. The same power

218

that once split Sinai now divides soul and spirit, bone and marrow. When He speaks, idols topple, false confidences crumble, and foundations are tested. His word is not gentle suggestion; it is seismic authority.

The Shaking of the Visible

Everything visible is vulnerable. Empires, institutions, reputations—all of it is topsoil over shifting fault lines. The Roman Empire thought itself eternal; its marble now lies in fragments. The temples of Greece are ruins; the ziggurats of Babylon are sand. Nations rise like mountains and fall like dunes. Only one kingdom endures.

Drive through the countryside and you'll see the sermon written in timber and rust. Farmhouses that once rang with laughter now sag into the earth. The roof caves, the porch tilts, vines claim the walls. Once they were someone's dream—now they are memorials of impermanence.

You can almost imagine him there, years ago— working extra shifts at the mill, tucking away dollars in a coffee can, sketching plans at the kitchen table by the glow of a single lamp. He measured boards in his mind long before he ever picked up a hammer. She saved for curtains, for a garden, for children's voices in the hallway. The day they broke ground, they believed they were building forever. And for a while, they did. The wood was fresh, the paint clean, the laughter real. But time and weather never rest. The paint faded, the planks warped, the wind sighed through broken panes. The dream became dust, and the dust preached: Nothing here lasts.

That is what happens to all we build for the visible world. The paint fades; the planks rot; the wind wins.

The shaking is not cruelty—it is mercy. God shakes what cannot last so that we will stop clinging to it. He unsettles the sand so that we will stand on the Rock. Every economic collapse, every cultural upheaval, every personal trial is a rehearsal for that final shaking when heaven and earth themselves will pass away and only Christ's kingdom will remain.

The Shaking of the Soul

The same principle holds in the heart. When God speaks, the soul trembles before it stabilizes. Conviction is an earthquake of grace. He dismantles false foundations—self-righteousness, pride, independence—so that the life of Christ can take root. We fear the shaking, but it is how God saves. Sinai's earthquake sent men running; Calvary's earthquake opened graves.

When Jesus died, the ground shook. When He rose, the stone rolled. When the Spirit descended, the place where they prayed was shaken. The kingdom always advances by tremor. Grace never leaves the landscape as it was.

Zinger: When God shakes you, He's not trying to bury you—He's trying to build you on something unshakable.

Psalm 46 sings of this same stability amid chaos:

"Though the earth be removed, and though the mountains be carried into the midst of the sea... God is in the midst of her; she shall not be moved."

The city of God is earthquake-proof not because there is no shaking, but because its foundations run deeper than the world's crust. Zion cannot fall because its cornerstone is Christ Himself.

The Shaking of the Heavens

Hebrews pushes further: God will not only shake the earth but also the heavens. The visible heavens—the sky, the stars, the galaxies—will one day ripple under His command. Peter describes it: *"The elements shall melt with fervent heat."* Revelation shows the sky rolling back like a scroll, the sun darkened, the stars falling. The entire physical universe will convulse in obedience to the Creator's final word. And out of that shaking will emerge something wholly new: "*a new heaven and a new earth, wherein dwelleth righteousness.*"

Creation began with a voice— "*Let there be light.*" It will end with a voice— "*Behold, I make all things new.*" The same Word that formed the worlds will finish them. The first shaking made matter; the final shaking will reveal meaning.

For the believer, this is not terror but triumph. We will not be cast down with the dust; we will rise with the kingdom. The shaking that destroys the counterfeit will display the authentic. Everything built on Christ will stand taller for having been tested. His voice does not merely tear down—it clears the ground for glory.

Receiving an Unshakable Kingdom

"Wherefore, we receiving a kingdom which cannot be moved..."

Daniel saw it long ago: a stone cut without hands smote the image of human empire and grew into a mountain filling the earth. That stone was Christ. The kingdoms of this world will be blown away like chaff, but His kingdom is forever.

Notice the wording: we receiving. It is present tense. The kingdom is not merely future; it is already ours in seed form. Every act of obedience is participation in the eternal. Every unseen labor for Christ is part of a realm that will never fall.

Therefore, *"let us have grace."*

The phrase is startling. It is not a command to **do** but to **be**—to remain in a posture of humble dependence. Grace is not something we grasp; it is something we stand in. We are not told to manufacture thankfulness or to project serenity; we are told to have grace—to hold our position on the rock of unearned favor.

I wrestled with that phrase: *let us have grace.* What does it mean to *have grace?* It is not passive resignation; it is active rest. To have grace is to live from the settled confidence that all strength, all safety, all sufficiency are already provided in Christ.

Those who know this grace serve God *"acceptably, with reverence and godly fear."* Grace and reverence are not opposites. Grace does not make God casual; it makes Him nearer, and therefore holier. When grace truly lands, worship deepens.

Our God Is a Consuming Fire

Hebrews closes this magnificent vision of the unshakable kingdom with a warning that glows like the mountain it describes:

> *"Wherefore we receiving a kingdom which cannot be moved, let us have grace, whereby we may serve God acceptably with reverence and godly fear: for our God is a consuming fire." (Heb. 12:28–29)*

The words fall heavy. Not, "our God was," nor "our God can be," but *"our God **is** a consuming fire."* He has not changed from Sinai to Zion. The same holiness that once set the mountain ablaze still burns with undiminished intensity. The difference is not in His nature but in our access. At Sinai, fire repelled; at Calvary, fire received. What terrified now transforms. The God who once descended in wrath now indwells in grace—but He remains fire all the same.

The Fire That Destroys and the Fire That Purifies

Fire is never neutral. It either devours or it refines, depending on what it touches. When it meets straw, it consumes; when it meets gold, it cleanses. So too with God's holiness. For the rebel, it is destruction; for the redeemed, purification. Judgment and sanctification are the same flame, working different outcomes.

The prophet Malachi saw it: *"He is like a refiner's fire... and He shall purify the sons of Levi."* The goal of that fire is not annihilation but holiness—burning away the alloy so that only the likeness of Christ remains. God does not burn His children in anger; He burns away everything that keeps them from His likeness.

The same fire that consumes sin refines saints.

The Fire of Presence

In Scripture, fire is always the emblem of divine presence. A flaming sword guarded Eden; a pillar of fire led Israel by night; fire descended on the altar in Leviticus and on the disciples at Pentecost. Every manifestation of fire marked the nearness of God. The closer we draw to Him, the more we feel the heat.

Our worship, then, is not casual attendance at a cosmic campfire—it is entering the blaze. To serve God "acceptably" means to step into that fire with reverence and godly fear, knowing that we approach One who is holy, not harmless. We do not tame Him; we trust Him. We do not manage His presence; we marvel in it.

The Fire That Cleans the Field

There's a farmer near our home who, every spring, burns off his fields. From the road, it looks like ruin— black smoke curling upward, the earth scorched and lifeless. But give it a week, and you'll see the miracle: bright green blades pushing through the ash. The fire has cleared away the rot and made room for growth. What looked like death was preparation for life.

So it is with the believer. When the Spirit's fire passes over the field of our hearts, He is not destroying us— He is clearing us. Pride, resentment, bitterness, envy —these are the weeds that choke the Word. The divine flame burns them away so that the seed of grace can flourish.

The Fire That Dwells Within

For the church, God's fire no longer blazes on a distant mountain—it burns within. The Holy Spirit is not a lesser flame but the same eternal fire, now inhabiting clay vessels. He refines us from the inside out. He ignites conviction, illuminates truth, and fuels love. To walk in the Spirit is to live aflame—to be steadily kindled toward likeness with Christ.

When we resist the Spirit, we cool. When we grieve Him, we smother the flame. But when we yield, the glow returns, the passion rekindles, and the presence of God fills the temple again.

The Fire That Welcomes

To say "our God is a consuming fire" is not to paint Him as cruel but as completely pure. Nothing impure can survive His presence, but everything surrendered is transformed by it. The consuming fire of God is the promise that evil will not have the final word, that sin will not linger forever, that the dross will not endure. One day, when He shakes the heavens and the earth, that fire will finish its work. Every trace of corruption will be gone, and what remains will shine like crystal in the light of the Lamb.

Until then, we live before that fire with reverence and grace. We do not shrink from it; we stay near it. The warmth that once terrified Israel now sustains us. The flame that once forbade approach now lights our way home.

Summary

Faith brings us to a mountain that cannot be touched yet is more real than the one that burned with fire. At Sinai, holiness terrified; at Zion, holiness transforms. The Old Covenant warned, "Stay back"; the New Covenant invites, "Come near." We have not come to thunder and smoke, but to the Mediator who bears the marks of peace. Yet the fire has not gone out—it has moved inside the believer.

The God who shook Sinai now shakes the soul, not to destroy but to purify. Every shaking removes the temporary so that the eternal may remain. Every flame that touches us removes dross and reveals grace. The church of the living God is not built on untested stone but on the Rock that endures every quake. In a collapsing world, we receive a kingdom that cannot be moved. The only fitting response is worship that trembles with awe and burns with gratitude.

Application

- **Lay aside the visible.** Do not pour your life into what time will take. Live for the unseen, eternal kingdom that cannot decay.

- **Listen when God shakes.** When He unsettles your comfort, He is not abandoning you—He is strengthening your foundation.

- **Welcome the fire.** Invite God's holiness to burn away pride, bitterness, and pretense, knowing His fire cleanses before it comforts.

- **Serve with reverence.** Approach worship as sacred ground. We serve not a manageable deity but a majestic King whose presence still burns.

- **Hold grace tightly.** "Let us have grace," says the writer—not only to receive it but to reflect it. Live graciously because you stand in grace.

- **Stand unshaken.** When the world trembles, remember: you belong to the kingdom that will outlast every storm, every empire, every age.

Prayer

Father,

You are holy beyond our comprehension and faithful beyond our deserving. We bow before You with reverence and godly fear, grateful that Your fire refines instead of consumes.

Burn away what cannot abide in Your presence. Shake from us every confidence that is not Christ, and make us steadfast upon the Rock that cannot be moved.

With Your Spirit, teach us to serve You acceptably—with humility, with gratitude, and with holy awe. Let our lives be living altars, glowing with obedience and grace. And when the heavens and the earth are shaken one last time, may we be found standing in the light of Your unshakable kingdom.

We pray these things in the name of Jesus,

Amen.

9

Love that Remains

The book of Hebrews ends not with thunder but with tenderness. After unveiling Christ as Priest, Mediator, and King of the unshakable kingdom, the writer closes with the quiet proof of faith —love lived out. The mountain that blazed with glory now glows with hearth-light. The final exhortations of chapter 13 show what it looks like when heavenly truth touches earthly life. Doctrine bends down into daily duty.

Brotherly Love Continues

"Let brotherly love continue." (v. 1)

The epistle's final chapter opens with one of the simplest and most searching commands in all Scripture. After twelve chapters of majestic doctrine—

Christ's priesthood, covenant, sacrifice, and kingdom —the writer brings the believer to a single test of understanding: Has love endured?

"Brotherly love" translates the Greek word *philadelphia*—affection between those who share the same family. It is not sentimentality but spiritual kinship. We are bound together by the same adoption, the same blood of atonement, the same indwelling Spirit. Love among believers is not elective; it is hereditary. To be born of God is to belong to His household, and to belong to His household is to love its members.

Love as the Fruit of Doctrine

This command appears not at the beginning of the letter, but at its end. The writer has led his readers through the thunder of Sinai, the mercy of Calvary, the glory of the heavenly sanctuary. Now he turns to the hearth. Doctrine culminates in devotion; theology must become tenderness. Truth that does not issue in love has not yet been believed. As Paul wrote, *"Though I understand all mysteries... and have not charity, I am nothing."*

The church had endured loss and persecution. Some had been expelled from synagogues; others had lost property or freedom. Hardship had drawn sharp edges between them. Weariness makes love difficult.

But precisely then comes the command: Let it continue. Keep what suffering tries to extinguish. The flame of affection must not die on the altar of endurance.

The Nature of Brotherly Love

Biblical love is not permissive tolerance; it is holy concern for another's eternal good. It is as ready to warn as to comfort, as willing to correct as to console. Modern religion often confuses love with affirmation, as if kindness required agreement. But God's love does not lie to us about sin; it tells us the truth to spare us destruction. *"Whom the Lord loveth He chasteneth."* In the same way, love within the church may rebuke as well as embrace. It protects truth for the sake of souls.

Yet love is also patient, gracious, and loyal. It bears long with weakness; it forgives seventy times seven; it seeks reconciliation where pride would rather retreat. Love does not measure what it gives or count what it loses. It remains when feelings fade, when gratitude fails, when reward never comes. To *"let brotherly love continue"* is to make affection a discipline rather than a mood—to keep choosing goodwill when emotion grows cold.

Love as the Evidence of Grace

This single verse summarizes the entire letter's moral theology: faith produces endurance, endurance produces holiness, and holiness produces love. Faith believes what God says; love behaves as God loves. The unshakable kingdom is not an empire of stone but a fellowship of hearts united in Christ. Brotherly love is its law, its culture, and its witness.

Jesus said, *"By this shall all men know that ye are My disciples, if ye have love one to another."* The world is not convinced by our arguments but by our affection. A church divided by resentment cannot preach reconciliation; a believer who hoards grace cannot speak of salvation. Love is not the garnish of Christian life—it is the proof of it.

The Continuance of Love

The verb *menetō* ("continue") conveys endurance and permanence. It does not command that love begin but that it not end. The church must guard love from erosion. It dies not in storms but in neglect. Bitterness, comparison, fatigue, or the small abrasions of daily life can cool the warmth that once bound believers together. Therefore the writer says, let it continue. Feed it. Defend it. Forgive quickly, pray constantly, and remember that the same blood bought the brother who wounded you.

Love's endurance is itself a miracle of grace. Human affection wanes; divine charity perseveres. The same Spirit who poured God's love into our hearts (Romans 5:5) now sustains it through trials, differences, and disappointments. When we are tempted to withdraw, He reminds us of the love that never withdrew from us.

The Hospitality of Love

"Be not forgetful to entertain strangers: for thereby some have entertained angels unawares." (v. 2)

Love that endures must also extend. The first expression of brotherly love in this chapter is hospitality—the willingness to open one's door and one's heart. In the early church, this command was not sentimental advice; it was a necessity. To forget hospitality was to forget humanity itself.

The Historical Setting

In the first century, travel was difficult and dangerous. There were few formal inns, and those that existed were infamous for vice, theft, and exploitation. Christian travelers—missionaries, merchants, and refugees alike—depended on the kindness of believers in every town. To welcome a stranger was to risk personal safety, reputation, and sometimes even property. Yet the gospel spread from home to home on the strength of such risk. Without open tables, there would have been no open hearts.

Persecution, however, had made the Hebrew believers cautious. They had suffered loss and rejection; some had been imprisoned; others had been ostracized by neighbors. Weariness makes the door creak when opened. "Be not forgetful," the writer says. The phrase assumes that hospitality had once been their habit but had grown rare. Fear and fatigue had dulled generosity. The church had grown wary of outsiders—and, in doing so, had begun to grow smaller within.

Hospitality as Worship

The call to hospitality is not mere social courtesy; it is a sacred act. To welcome a guest in Christ's name is to recognize the image of God in another soul. The Greek term translated entertain strangers (*philoxenia*) literally means "love of the foreigner." It is the counterpart of *philadelphia*, love of the brother. Love of the brother keeps the family together; love of the stranger invites the lost in. Both are necessary for the kingdom to grow.

Hospitality, then, is an extension of divine character. God is Himself the great Host, spreading a table in the wilderness and inviting the undeserving to dine. Every believer who opens the door repeats that gospel in miniature. A warm meal, a clean bed, a listening ear—these are sacraments of kindness, earthly signs of heavenly welcome.

Angels Unawares

The writer strengthens his appeal with one of Scripture's most curious and comforting promises: *"For thereby some have entertained angels unawares."* The reference recalls Abraham, who ran to meet three travelers near the oaks of Mamre, bowing low before them, washing their feet, and hastening to prepare a meal. Only later did he discover that one of them was the Lord Himself and the others His angels. Lot, too, welcomed two men into his home at Sodom, protecting them at peril to his life, and found that he had sheltered messengers of heaven.

The principle is not that every guest is an angel, but that every act of hospitality touches the realm of the divine. God often disguises His messengers in need so that our love may be tested in humility. The poor, the weary, the overlooked—they carry heaven's credentials unseen. The believer who opens the door to them finds, afterward, that the blessing flows both directions.

The Spiritual Reward

Hospitality blesses both giver and receiver. The host finds that generosity loosens the grip of self; the guest discovers that grace still has human hands. In welcoming others, we welcome Christ Himself, who said, *"I was a stranger, and ye took Me in."* The measure of our love is not how warmly we greet friends, but how kindly we serve those who can offer nothing in return.

A closed heart leads to a closed door; an open door keeps the heart alive. The church that forgets hospitality forgets its own story, for we were all strangers whom God welcomed. The gospel began with divine hospitality—God inviting sinners to the table of grace. Every Christian home that practices the same writes another chapter in that eternal welcome.

The Empathy of Love

"Remember them that are in bonds, as bound with them; and them which suffer adversity, as being yourselves also in the body." (v. 3)

Love that continues and welcomes must also remember.

The writer now turns from hospitality to empathy— from the open door to the shared burden. The early church knew what it meant to suffer. Some had been cast into prison for confessing Christ; others had lost possessions, reputation, or family. Those who remained free were tempted to turn inward—to protect themselves by forgetting the afflicted. But love cannot be content with safety while a brother suffers in chains.

To Remember Is to Act

In Scripture, remembering is never passive. When God "remembered Noah," He sent a wind to dry the flood. When He "remembered Rachel," He opened her womb. Divine remembrance always moves toward deliverance. So when the Holy Spirit commands, *"Remember them that are in bonds,"* He is not asking for sentiment but for solidarity. We are to remember in prayer, in provision, and, when possible, in presence.

The phrase *as bound with them* demands more than pity—it demands identification. We are not to view the imprisoned believer as a stranger enduring misfortune, but as a member of our own body. Their chains are our chains. Their cell is our cell. When one member suffers, all suffer with it (1 Cor. 12:26). The Church is not a collection of individuals; it is one organism animated by one Spirit. If the hand is shackled, the whole body feels the pull.

Empathy as Incarnation

The pattern for such compassion is Christ Himself. The Son of God remembered those bound in sin and entered their bondage to free them. He did not save us from a distance; He came where we were, *"touched with the feeling of our infirmities"* (Heb. 4:15). To remember the suffering as *"being yourselves also in the body"* is to imitate that incarnate mercy. We stoop to lift because He stooped to save.

Empathy is one of love's hardest disciplines. It asks us to feel pain that is not our own, to enter darkness we could avoid. Yet nothing displays the character of Christ more vividly than compassionate identification.

When we kneel beside the broken, we stand beside the Savior.

The Cost of Forgetfulness

Indifference is easier. When persecution grows fierce or need becomes overwhelming, self-protection whispers, "It's not your burden." But to forget the suffering church is to deny the body of Christ. The believers to whom this letter was written had once shown remarkable compassion: *"Ye took joyfully the spoiling of your goods, knowing that ye have in heaven a better and an enduring substance."* (Heb. 10:34) But fear had dulled their zeal. The writer now calls them back to that earlier courage. To love is to remember; to forget is to drift from grace.

Even in less perilous times, this command pierces us. The imprisoned and the persecuted still fill the earth; the lonely and the overlooked sit silently beside us. Love does not measure suffering by geography or publicity. It stoops where it finds pain and says, "You are not forgotten."

The Practical Outworking

To remember those in bonds may mean writing letters, visiting, providing for families left behind, or lifting continual intercession for those enduring hardship. It may mean slowing our pace to walk beside the wounded, choosing inconvenience over indifference. The church is never more Christlike than when it bears another's cross.

Empathy as the Heart of the Kingdom

The unshakable kingdom is built not on strength but on sympathy. The King who reigns is the same Shepherd who suffered. To belong to His realm is to share His heart. A community that feels each other's pain becomes unshakable, for no storm can scatter those whose souls are knit together in compassion. The world recognizes such love as something foreign, something heavenly—a love that bleeds, yet does not break.

"Bear ye one another's burdens, and so fulfil the law of Christ." (Gal. 6:2)

The Fidelity of Love

The Holy Spirit moves from brotherly affection to covenantal fidelity. Love that continues and cares must also remain pure. The writer's tone shifts from tenderness to firmness, for the same grace that teaches compassion also guards holiness. The heart that opens to others must first be faithful to the one with whom it has made covenant.

Marriage Declared, Not Debated

In the original Greek, this verse contains no verbs of command—no "let it be" or "should be." It is not an exhortation but a declaration: "*Marriage **is** honorable in all.*" God has spoken. The institution does not depend upon human approval or cultural trend; it rests upon divine design. Long before the Law, before Israel, before sin entered the world, marriage was God's idea—one man, one woman, joined by God Himself.

In a world where vows are made lightly and broken easily, this statement stands like a monument: Marriage is honorable. Not optional, not outdated, not a mere arrangement of convenience—but sacred, enduring, and central to the moral order of creation. When society forgets that, it forgets itself.

The Sanctity of Union

The marriage bed is declared undefiled. Physical intimacy, within the covenant God ordained, is not shameful but sacred. It is the language of self-giving love, the earthly echo of divine communion. What the world twists into indulgence, God intended as worship. To keep the bed pure is to guard the symbol of Christ and His church—a union marked by fidelity and grace.

The purity of marriage protects more than individuals; it preserves families, generations, and faith itself. A home rooted in covenant faithfulness becomes a sanctuary where truth and tenderness dwell together. Children learn from it the meaning of steadfast love; the church sees in it the reflection of its Redeemer's faithfulness. To dishonor marriage, therefore, is not merely to sin against a spouse but to desecrate a divine picture.

The Judgment of the Unfaithful

"But whoremongers and adulterers God will judge." This warning, stark and unsoftened, carries the same authority as the preceding blessing. The God who sanctifies also judges. In the pagan world surrounding the early church, immorality was so common that fidelity seemed almost eccentric. The Christian home, chaste and committed, shone like a lamp in a darkened street. The writer reminds believers that God's standards have not shifted with the culture. Sin remains sin, not because God is cruel but because He is kind.

Every moral boundary He draws is a protection, not a prison. When humanity transgresses, the judgment that follows is often natural consequence rather than supernatural curse: hearts scarred, trust broken, intimacy poisoned, joy lost. Sin promises ecstasy and delivers emptiness. The pleasure fades, but the pain remains.

Fidelity as Worship

Faithfulness in marriage is more than ethics; it is theology. Every vow kept is a living testimony of God's covenant-keeping nature. In every generation, Christian marriage declares anew that the Lord never forsakes His own. The husband's steadfast love mirrors Christ's devotion to His church; the wife's faithful respect reflects the church's reverent submission to Christ. Where fidelity reigns, the gospel is preached without words.

A Call to Reverence

The writer's tone throughout Hebrews has exalted Christ as our High Priest—the One who mediates between holiness and humanity. Now, in this single verse, he calls every believer to live as a priest within the home—offering purity as a continual sacrifice. The marriage bed becomes an altar of mutual honor;

the home, a sanctuary where covenant love burns like the lamp of the tabernacle, never to be extinguished.

The unshakable kingdom is upheld by such faithfulness. Where marriage is despised, the foundation of society trembles; but where it is revered, the flame of divine order still glows.

Marriage is honourable in all.

Let no culture, fashion, or folly persuade us otherwise.

The Contentment of Love

"Let your conversation be without covetousness; and be content with such things as ye have: for He hath said, I will never leave thee, nor forsake thee." (v. 5)

Love that is faithful must also be content. The writer moves from the covenant of the home to the condition of the heart. Fidelity guards what we have; contentment rejoices in it. Both are expressions of trust in a faithful God. If love is to remain pure toward others, it must first rest secure in Him.

The Quiet Virtue

Contentment is among the rarest and most radiant of Christian virtues. It is not complacency or laziness, nor does it despise effort or ambition. It is the settled assurance that one already possesses, in Christ, everything that truly matters. The discontented soul cannot love well—it is too busy counting what it lacks. Covetousness breeds comparison; comparison breeds resentment; resentment poisons fellowship. A jealous heart cannot rejoice with those who rejoice.

So the Spirit commands: "Let your conversation," that is, your way of life, "be without covetousness." Greed is not confined to money. We covet applause, comfort, position, and ease. Discontent can wear a thousand faces—envy at another's success, restlessness with our own calling, or bitterness over what God has withheld. Each form whispers the same accusation: God has not been good enough to me. To be content is to silence that lie with gratitude.

Discontent questions God's goodness; contentment trusts it.

The Presence That Satisfies

The command is immediately joined to a promise: *"For He hath said, I will never leave thee, nor forsake thee."* The Greek contains five negatives—an emphatic *"I will never, never, never, never, never leave you."* The antidote to covetousness is not **possession** but **presence**. The soul that knows it is accompanied by God no longer feels impoverished.

Every anxious grasping after "more" begins in a sense of aloneness—an unspoken fear that we are left to provide for ourselves. But when the believer rests in the Lord's companionship, striving turns to serenity. Contentment grows not from abundance of goods but from awareness of grace. You may lose employment, comfort, even reputation, but you cannot lose Emmanuel—God with us. That promise steadies trembling hands and quiets restless hearts.

The Boldness of Dependence

"So that we may boldly say, The Lord is my helper, and I will not fear what man shall do unto me." Contentment does not make us passive; it makes us fearless. The one who depends upon God alone can no longer be manipulated by men. Money cannot bribe him; threat cannot bend him. He is free because his security is already settled. This is the secret of Paul's joy in prison and the serenity of martyrs at the stake: "The Lord is my helper."

The believer who learns contentment becomes unshakable, not because he possesses everything but because he has ceased to be possessed by anything. His treasures are in heaven, beyond theft or decay. His peace cannot be purchased and therefore cannot be stolen.

The Fellowship of Contentment

Discontent isolates, but gratitude gathers. A contented church is a peaceful church, free from rivalry and resentment. When believers rest in the provision of God, they can rejoice in the blessings of others without envy. Gratitude builds fellowship where greed breeds suspicion. Love flourishes best in a heart that has ceased to compare.

The Christ of Contentment

Ultimately, this command is not about simplicity of lifestyle but about sufficiency in Christ. The writer has spent the entire letter proving that Jesus is enough— better than angels, better than Moses, better than Aaron, better than the world's systems and securities. To close with "be content" is to apply that truth personally. If He is all-sufficient, then we lack nothing that love requires.

The unshakable kingdom does not promise unending wealth, but unbroken fellowship. Its citizens find joy not in what they hold but in Whose hands they rest.

"The Lord is my helper."

That is the song of the contented heart—the love that has ceased striving because it has found its source.

The Respect of Love

"Remember them which have the rule over you, who have spoken unto you the word of God: whose faith follow, considering the end of their conversation." (v. 7)

Love expresses itself not only in fellowship among equals but in reverence toward those who lead. Having taught believers to love one another, to open their homes, to share in one another's burdens, and to live contentedly before God, the writer now exhorts them to remember and respect those who have labored among them in the Word.

The command to "remember" once again implies active gratitude, not passive recollection. These leaders were not political figures but spiritual shepherds—men who had "spoken unto you the word of God." Their influence was not in personality or position but in proclamation. They had shaped the church by faithfully unfolding Scripture, guiding the flock by the light of truth rather than the shadow of opinion.

Honoring the Faithful

The early believers had known leaders who paid dearly for their faith. Some had already died for the gospel; others had endured persecution, imprisonment, and reproach. The writer calls the church to reflect on their example: "Whose faith follow, considering the end of their conversation." The "end" here refers not merely to death but to the outcome—the fruit of a life well lived and a death well died. The call is not to idolize their memory but to imitate their perseverance.

True spiritual leadership always points away from itself to Christ. The best leaders are not those who build their own following but those who cultivate disciples of Jesus. Their legacy is measured not in influence but in integrity, not in fame but in faithfulness.

The Spirit of Obedience

To remember such leaders is to value the Word they taught, to preserve the truth they handed down, and to walk in the path they opened. This is not blind allegiance but grateful continuity. The believer honors his leaders best not by quoting them but by continuing in the doctrine they loved. The church that forgets its faithful pastors soon forgets its faithful Lord.

Leadership in the body of Christ is never absolute. The shepherd has no authority apart from the Word of God, and the flock has no safety apart from submission to that Word. When both remain under Scripture, harmony thrives. The Spirit who anoints the preacher also illuminates the hearer; together they grow into maturity under the same Head—Christ Himself.

The Unchanging Christ

The call to remember faithful leaders flows directly into one of the most comforting verses in all Scripture: "Jesus Christ the same yesterday, and today, and for ever." The faith of the past remains relevant because its object has not changed. The gospel is not an evolving idea; it is the revelation of an unchanging Savior. Leaders may come and go, churches may rise and fall, but Christ remains constant—the same Shepherd who called them calls us still.

The verse also guards against misplaced dependence. When a beloved pastor dies or a generation passes, the temptation is to feel orphaned. But the writer reassures the church: the Christ who sustained your fathers sustains you. Their faith was not in their own courage but in His constancy. He is the same Lord who spoke to Abraham, strengthened Paul, comforted persecuted saints, and now indwells

His people. His truth does not age, His promises do not expire, His love does not wane.

Love and Leadership

The unshakable kingdom is not built on personalities but on permanence. Leadership in the church is a relay, not a throne. Each generation receives the baton of truth and carries it forward until Christ returns. To respect our leaders, therefore, is to participate in that sacred continuity—to keep running faithfully in the same direction, guided by the same Lord.

The love that honors authority also anchors itself in eternity. It looks beyond the frailty of human shepherds to the everlasting Shepherd who never resigns, never fails, and never changes. His voice still calls through every faithful pulpit: "Follow Me."

The Faithfulness of Love

"Be not carried about with divers and strange doctrines." (v. 9)

Every generation of believers faces two dangers: the chill of neglect and the drift of novelty. The writer, having exhorted the church to remember its faithful teachers and to look to the unchanging Christ, now warns against the fickleness of new ideas that claim deeper insight but deliver only confusion. The faith that endures must be anchored, not adrift.

The Seduction of the New

The phrase "divers and strange doctrines" refers to teachings foreign to the gospel—doctrines that may sound spiritual but lack the substance of grace. In the first century, Jewish believers were tempted to blend the freedom of Christ with the regulations of the Law, reintroducing ritual diets and ceremonial observances as marks of holiness. Others were drawn to speculative mysticism, imagining hidden knowledge beyond the plain truth of the Word.

Such teachings appeal to pride. They promise progress but produce instability. The believer who runs after novelty soon forgets the sufficiency of Christ. The heart becomes like a ship without ballast —impressive in motion, but destined to capsize. What was once conviction becomes curiosity; what was once worship becomes wandering.

The Steadfast Heart

"It is a good thing that the heart be established with grace." Here lies the antidote. The stability of the Christian life does not depend on accumulating knowledge or multiplying rules, but on resting in the unmerited favor of God. Grace roots the soul. It keeps us from both arrogance and anxiety—from the pride that says "I have achieved" and the fear that says "I must perform."

To be "established" means to be settled, anchored, no longer tossed by tides of emotion or argument. Grace is not only the entrance to salvation but its environment. The believer grows in the same soil in which he was planted. As Paul wrote, "As ye have therefore received Christ Jesus the Lord, so walk ye in Him." We were saved by grace; we stand by grace; we serve by grace.

The Futility of Ritual

The writer contrasts grace with "meats"—the ceremonial foods prescribed under the Mosaic law. These dietary distinctions had once served as visual lessons of holiness, but now that Christ had come, they were obsolete. Those who returned to such shadows "had not profited." The outward regulation could not produce inward renewal. Rituals can restrain behavior but never redeem the heart. Only grace transforms from the inside out.

Religion without grace quickly becomes superstition—rules without relationship, performance without peace. The Old Covenant law was good, but it could not make its followers good. The sacrifices of animals and the abstaining from foods were temporary scaffolding; grace is the finished temple.

Faithfulness Guarded by Grace

Love and truth walk together. To love God rightly, we must believe rightly; to love others faithfully, we must stand firmly in grace. A drifting doctrine soon produces a decaying devotion. The believer who forgets grace becomes harsh toward others or hopeless toward himself. But the one whose heart is established by grace loves patiently, forgives freely, and stands unshaken amid controversy.

The unshakable kingdom is not held together by novelty but by necessity—the necessity of grace. Every fresh movement that claims to "improve" upon the gospel eventually discovers that it has left the gospel behind. There is nothing newer than Christ resurrected, and nothing older than His covenant love.

The Faithful Balance

The writer's warning is not against thought but against instability. The mature believer remains curious but not credulous, discerning but not cynical. He tests all things by Scripture and holds fast that which is good. He knows that truth is not fragile—it invites examination—but he also knows that grace is the test of truth. Any teaching that diminishes Christ or divides His people is not from heaven, no matter how eloquent the argument.

To be faithful in love is to be faithful in truth, and to be faithful in truth is to stay centered in grace. Love built on any other foundation will collapse under the weight of fear or pride.

"It is a good thing that the heart be established with grace."

That is the anchor of the unshakable life.

The Sacrifice of Love

"We have an altar, whereof they have no right to eat which serve the tabernacle... Wherefore Jesus also, that He might sanctify the people with His own blood, suffered without the gate. Let us go forth therefore unto Him without the camp, bearing His reproach." (vv. 10–13)

257

The Christian's Altar

Having just warned against empty ritual and manmade religion, the writer now proclaims the glorious reality that the believer does have an altar— but not one of stone or brass. Our altar is Christ Himself. The imagery shifts from the fading temple in Jerusalem to the eternal sanctuary in heaven. The priests who continued to serve the tabernacle had no right to this altar because they clung to shadows after the Substance had appeared.

The Old Covenant priest stood beside an altar that smoked with continual sacrifice. He could eat from many of those offerings, sharing in the meal that symbolized peace between God and man. But not from the sin offering. The bodies of those animals were burned outside the camp. The sin offering was the most holy of all, and its blood was brought into the Holy of Holies once a year for atonement. Its flesh was never eaten. It was consumed entirely by fire, representing judgment borne away.

Now the writer declares: that sacrifice was only a figure. The true sin offering has come—the Lamb of God who takes away the sin of the world. His altar is the cross; His blood the everlasting covenant; His flesh not burned but broken. Every believer who trusts in Him feeds upon that altar, partaking of the benefits of His death through faith.

The Horror and the Holiness

"Wherefore Jesus also, that He might sanctify the people with His own blood, suffered without the gate." The picture here is deliberate and shocking. The most holy sacrifice was taken to the most unholy place. Outside the gate was the city dump—the refuse of Jerusalem, the stench of rot and smoke, the cries of the condemned. There the Lamb of God was slain.

The writer of Hebrews wants us to feel the contrast: holiness carried to humiliation, majesty dragged through muck, purity thrown into the filth of sin's waste pile. Why? That He might sanctify the people. Our cleansing was purchased not in the courts of gold but in the gutters of Golgotha. He was the sin offering consumed outside the camp, under the open sky, under the full weight of wrath. The horror of the cross revealed the holiness of our God and the gravity of our guilt.

The Call to Go Forth

"Let us go forth therefore unto Him without the camp, bearing His reproach." The Christian life is not lived in the comfort of acceptance but in the fellowship of rejection. The "camp" represents the safety of conformity—the religious system that prefers respectability to righteousness, ritual to repentance.

To go "without the camp" is to leave behind every false security, to identify openly with the crucified Christ, and to bear the shame of His name before the world.

It is one thing to admire Jesus from a distance; it is another to walk with Him in reproach. Love must move us. The same love that drew Him outside the gate draws us after Him. The cross is both our altar and our calling. To follow Jesus is to exchange the praise of men for the presence of God.

The Fire of Consecration

In Israel, the bodies burned outside the camp were a visible reminder that sin was costly and holiness was costly. Every flicker of fire declared that guilt demanded judgment. When Christ died outside the gate, He bore the full flame of divine wrath in our stead. But that fire which once destroyed now purifies. The believer who follows Christ outside the camp is not consumed but consecrated. The same fire that burned against sin now burns within the heart —holy zeal for a holy Savior.

To love Christ truly is to share His reproach, to embrace His cross, and to count it joy. This is the sacrifice of love: to offer ourselves willingly in the service of the One who offered Himself for us.

"Let us go forth therefore unto Him..."

The altar calls. The camp fades. The cross stands. And love walks out to meet Him there.

The Expectation of Love

"For here have we no continuing city, but we seek one to come." (Hebrews 13:14)

The Passing City

The writer's imagery shifts from the wilderness camp of Israel to the walled city of Jerusalem. In the Jewish mind, that city represented permanence—the dwelling place of God, the center of worship, the pride of the nation.   Yet by the time this epistle was written, Jerusalem was only a few years away from destruction.   The temple would fall, its stones scattered, its altars silenced.   What men called "everlasting" would soon lie in ruins.

This verse captures the essence of pilgrimage faith. The Christian has no continuing city—not because he has no home, but because his home is still ahead. Everything built by human hands eventually decays. Empires crumble, houses collapse, even churches grow old and fade. We are not meant to settle in the visible; we are meant to travel toward the invisible.

The Heart of the Pilgrim

Love loosens our grip on earth. When we love the eternal, we begin to see the temporary for what it is—a season, a shadow, a stewardship. Abraham "looked for a city which hath foundations, whose builder and maker is God." He lived in tents, not because he loved discomfort, but because he loved destiny. He believed that what God was building was better than anything man could preserve.

The believer today must learn the same rhythm of faith. We work, we build, we plan—but not as though these things will last forever. Every blessing is borrowed; every possession is temporary. Our task is to live as stewards, not settlers. The earth is not our inheritance; Christ is.

The Fading and the Forever

"Here we have no continuing city." That phrase reads like an obituary over every earthly dream. The skyscrapers of our age will someday look like the ruins of Babylon; the nations that seem invincible will someday be names in a history book. Even the strongest human bond—marriage, friendship, family—is fragile compared to eternity.

But we seek one to come. The word "*seek*" is active. We are not simply waiting for heaven; we are walking toward it. Every act of obedience, every step of faith, every tear shed for righteousness' sake is a movement toward that city. Heaven is not escapism —it is direction. The pilgrim heart is not weary of the world but oriented toward a better one.

The City of the Lamb

The "city to come" is not merely a place; it is a Person. It is the dwelling of God with His people, the fulfillment of every longing that faith has ever felt. Revelation describes it as the New Jerusalem—no temple, for the Lord God Almighty and the Lamb are the temple thereof; no sun, for the glory of God lightens it. Its streets are gold, not because of wealth, but because nothing there will rust or rot or ruin. It is the city that cannot be shaken, the homeland of the unshakable kingdom.

To love Christ is to long for that city. The saints of old confessed that they were strangers and pilgrims on the earth. Their hearts were already homesick for heaven. They were not fleeing from the world—they were following the Builder. Every loss, every hardship, every reproach endured "outside the camp" was a reminder that they were heading home.

The Expectation that Purifies

The expectation of love does not make us idle; it makes us holy. "Every man that hath this hope in him purifieth himself, even as He is pure." The pilgrim who knows where he is going walks differently. His eyes are lifted. His steps are lighter. His priorities are eternal. He can endure reproach, poverty, and misunderstanding because he measures life by eternity's horizon.

The Journey's End

This is the heartbeat of Hebrews: Don't go back. Go on. Don't return to the old city, the old sacrifices, the old securities. The temple is crumbling, but the kingdom stands. Love does not anchor itself in what fades; it fixes its hope in what is forever. To walk with Jesus "outside the camp" is to already be walking toward Zion. The gates of that city are open to those who bear His reproach with joy and who count no loss too great for His sake.

"Here we have no continuing city."

That is the humility of faith.

"We seek one to come."

264

That is the triumph of love.

The Praise of Love

"By Him therefore let us offer the sacrifice of praise to God continually, that is, the fruit of our lips giving thanks to His name." (v. 15)

The Continuation of Sacrifice

The writer has spoken of altars and offerings, of priests and blood. Yet he closes the thought not with the end of sacrifice, but with its transformation. The cross has not abolished worship—it has purified it. No longer do believers bring animals or grain; we bring ourselves. The Levitical priesthood ended, but the priesthood of praise began.

The phrase "By him therefore..." is crucial. Worship apart from Christ is noise. Only through His mediation can we approach God. He is both altar and priest, both sacrifice and song. When we praise, we come by Him—our melody carried by His merit. The fire that once consumed the lamb now kindles the believer's heart.

The Sacrifice of Praise

In the Old Testament, praise was often a shouted acclamation offered after deliverance. Here, it becomes the believer's daily offering because of deliverance. "The sacrifice of praise" is not confined to moments of triumph but offered continually—when the day is bright and when the night is long. Praise given in pain is the purest worship.

The "fruit of our lips" recalls the prophet Hosea's plea, "So will we render the calves of our lips." Words of gratitude have replaced the blood of bulls. Thanksgiving has taken the place of burnt offerings. The believer's mouth becomes an altar where truth is spoken, thanksgiving rises, and God is glorified. To praise God is not to flatter Him; it is to bear witness that He is faithful.

The Test of Sincerity

But praise that remains in the mouth is incomplete. Verse 16 follows naturally: "But to do good and to communicate forget not." The worship God delights in is not confined to melody but manifested in mercy. To "communicate" (Greek *koinōneō*) means to share—to hold nothing too tightly, whether possessions, time, or compassion.

Worship that ends with a song is unfinished; true praise always moves from the sanctuary to the street. The one who has tasted grace becomes gracious. The one who has been forgiven becomes forgiving. The one who has received blessing becomes a blessing. God measures our praise not only by how loudly we sing, but by how generously we serve.

The Pleasure of God

"With such sacrifices God is well pleased." That phrase—*well pleased*—is temple language. Under the Old Covenant, only a spotless lamb could please God. Under the new, it is the heart washed by grace and overflowing with gratitude. Every act of generosity, every word of kindness, every quiet deed done for His sake is incense on the altar of heaven. The smallest gift given in love becomes an act of cosmic significance when offered through Christ.

This is the priesthood of the believer: to live a life that smells like praise. The believer's home, workplace, and fellowship become holy ground when love is the fragrance and gratitude the flame. God delights in such worship—not because He needs it, but because it reflects His own heart. He is the Giver, and when His children give, His image shines.

The Unshakable Song

The "sacrifice of praise" belongs to the unshakable kingdom. Earthly temples crumble; choirs fall silent; altars decay. But praise outlasts them all. Long after the stars fade, the redeemed will still be singing. Their song will not be about their endurance but about His. Every act of obedience and every moment of thanksgiving rehearses eternity's anthem: 'Worthy is the Lamb that was slain."

Love that praises becomes love that serves. Love that serves becomes love that endures. The fire that fell on Calvary now burns in grateful hearts, and the smoke of their praise still rises before the throne.

The Generosity of Love

"But to do good and to communicate forget not: for with such sacrifices God is well pleased." (v. 16)

Love's praise must move from lips to hands. The God who delights in our worship delights also in our generosity. To "communicate" means to share—time, possessions, compassion. Giving is not loss; it is likeness to Christ, who gave Himself. Such sacrifices are not demanded by law but inspired by love. They please God because they resemble His Son.

268

The Submission of Love

"Obey them that have the rule over you, and submit yourselves: for they watch for your souls, as they that must give account." (v. 17)

The Shepherd's Charge

The letter to the Hebrews closes not with ceremony but with community. Having lifted our eyes to the heavenly city and called us to continual praise, the writer now turns to the order of life within the earthly fellowship. Faith must be lived somewhere, and that "somewhere" is the church. The kingdom is unshakable, but its citizens still need shepherds.

The word "rule" can sound harsh to modern ears, but in the Greek (*hēgeomai*), it carries the sense of guidance rather than governance. The church's leaders are not overlords but watchmen—those who stand on the wall and keep watch for the enemy's approach. They bear the weight of spiritual care, not the badge of superiority. They are answerable to Christ, the Chief Shepherd, whose flock they tend.

The pastor's authority is borrowed; the accountability is his own.

The Call to Trust

"Obey them that have the rule over you, and submit yourselves." These two commands are distinct yet complementary. Obey refers to the willingness to be persuaded—to give the leader's counsel a hearing shaped by humility. Submit means to yield—to allow oneself to be guided rather than insisting on self-direction. It does not call for blind allegiance, but for cooperative faith. The believer is not to follow a man instead of Christ, but to follow Christ through the man whom He has called.

Every healthy church rests on this mutual relationship: a leader who loves enough to speak truth, and a people who love enough to listen. When either fails, joy fades. Leadership becomes weary, and fellowship becomes brittle.

The Weight of Watching

"For they watch for your souls, as they that must give account." That phrase should make both pastor and people pause. The pastor's task is not merely to manage programs or maintain peace but to watch for souls. He stands between danger and the flock. He prays over them, teaches them, weeps for them, and, when necessary, confronts them. He must one day stand before God and answer for how he did so.

This is why spiritual leadership is not a matter of personal preference but of divine calling. The shepherd who fears men will fail to warn them; the one who fears God will speak the truth in love. And the congregation that honors that calling shares in its reward.

The Joy of Partnership

"That they may do it with joy, and not with grief." The tone here is tender. The writer does not demand submission to protect the leader's comfort but to preserve the congregation's blessing. A joyful shepherd is a fruitful shepherd. When the church family walks in unity—when members pray for their pastors, follow their guidance, and bear one another's burdens—the gospel advances with power. When strife or suspicion sets in, the church stalls.

Hebrews says bluntly, "for that is unprofitable for you." A church that grieves its leaders grieves the Spirit. Bitterness chokes ministry; joy multiplies it. The people who make their shepherd's work a delight will find themselves living under the overflow of that joy.

The Submission of Love

True submission in the body of Christ is not servitude but shared surrender—each member, pastor and people alike, yielding to the will of the same Lord. Authority in the church is not a hierarchy of importance but a hierarchy of responsibility. The one who leads bears the heavier yoke, and those who follow lighten it by their trust.

Love expresses itself not only in affection but in cooperation. To submit to godly leadership is to acknowledge that Christ still governs His church through human vessels. It is to believe that He has placed you within a family where accountability is grace, not bondage.

The unshakable kingdom is not built by one man's strength, but by many hearts submitted to one Lord.

The Benediction of Love

"Now the God of peace, that brought again from the dead our Lord Jesus, that great Shepherd of the sheep, through the blood of the everlasting covenant, make you perfect in every good work to do his will, working in you that which is well pleasing in his sight, through

Jesus Christ; to whom be glory for ever and ever. Amen." (Hebrews 13:20–21)

The God of Peace

After twelve chapters of exhortation and warning, the writer now rests the reader in benediction. The storm gives way to sunlight. "Now the God of peace..." — that title is not casual. It reminds us that the same God who thundered from Sinai now speaks from Zion, not in terror but in tenderness. Peace is His covenant signature. The Law revealed His justice; the gospel reveals His reconciliation.

This peace is not mere quiet or sentiment—it is wholeness. It means the war between God and man is over, not because man surrendered, but because Christ triumphed. The One who bore wrath now bestows rest. The altar still smokes, but it burns with the fire of fellowship, not fury.

The Shepherd Who Died and Rose

The God of peace is also the God of power—He "brought again from the dead our Lord Jesus." The resurrection is not an appendix to the gospel but its axis. The Shepherd lives. He did not merely lay down His life; He took it up again. Death could not hold the One who holds the keys of death and hell.

The writer calls Him 'that great Shepherd of the sheep." The imagery is personal. The Shepherd knows His sheep by name, and His care continues beyond the cross. He leads not from behind but from within—indwelling His flock by His Spirit. He guides through valleys, guards through danger, and gathers those who stray.

The Everlasting Covenant

This peace and power flow "through the blood of the everlasting covenant." The Old Covenant was sealed with the blood of bulls and goats—temporary, repetitive, and symbolic. The New Covenant is sealed with the blood of the Lamb—final, sufficient, and eternal. What began at Calvary will never be annulled. God's promises are as durable as the blood that guarantees them.

Every believer stands beneath that covenant. It is not a truce waiting to be broken but a relationship secured forever. The cross was not a temporary fix; it was an everlasting foundation. The same blood that saved you keeps you. The Shepherd who bled for His sheep will never abandon them.

The Work of Sanctification

"Make you perfect in every good work to do His will." The verb make perfect (*katartizō*) means "to mend, to equip, to make fit." It is the word used for setting a broken bone or outfitting a ship for voyage. God's goal is not merely to pardon us but to prepare us—to restore what sin fractured and to ready us for service. Every good work is a thread in the tapestry of His will.

The marvel is that He not only commands obedience but creates it: "working in you that which is well pleasing in His sight." Divine expectation is matched by divine enablement. The Shepherd not only leads His sheep to green pastures; He strengthens their legs to follow. Grace does not merely forgive failure— it fuels faithfulness.

The Glory of the Lamb

All of this is "through Jesus Christ; to whom be glory for ever and ever." The benediction closes as all true theology should—with doxology. The goal of salvation is not comfort but glory: that Christ might be magnified in His redeemed people. Every act of obedience, every offering of praise, every work done in love reflects the light of His eternal splendor.

This glory is not shared equally; it is shared reflectively. We do not compete with Christ's

275

radiance; we catch it. We are mirrors of mercy, not sources of it. The Shepherd's glory is our gladness, and His pleasure our purpose.

The Benediction of Love

The unshakable kingdom rests in the unchanging Christ. The covenant sealed in His blood is eternal, and the peace He brings is permanent. Love's benediction is not a dismissal but a commissioning. The God who has reconciled us now sends us—to live as citizens of His kingdom, ambassadors of His grace, and instruments of His glory.

The book of Hebrews began with God speaking through His Son. It ends with that same Son working through His saints.

"To whom be glory for ever and ever. Amen."

The Closing Appeal and Farewell

"And I beseech you, brethren, suffer the word of exhortation: for I have written a letter unto you in few words. Know ye that our brother Timothy is set at liberty; with whom, if he come shortly, I will see you. Salute all them that have the rule over you, and all the saints. They of

Italy salute you. Grace be with you all. Amen."
(Hebrews 13:22–25)

The Word of Exhortation

After one of the most profound theological treatises in Scripture, the writer ends with humility. "Suffer the word of exhortation." The phrase means "bear with this message." It acknowledges that truth can be heavy, that correction is rarely comfortable, and that endurance is required not only in suffering but in listening.

Hebrews is a demanding book. It calls believers to perseverance, maturity, purity, and faith that endures fire. Yet the writer's tone here is pastoral, not authoritarian. He pleads as a brother, not as a superior. Exhortation is not scolding but shepherding. It is love dressed in urgency. His "few words" may have felt long to his readers, but they were few compared to eternity.

The Fellowship of the Faithful

"Know ye that our brother Timothy is set at liberty; with whom, if he come shortly, I will see you." This brief note is more than a personal update—it reminds us that even the greatest apostles needed companionship. The unshakable kingdom is not built by isolated saints but by a family of faith. Paul (if he is the author) mentions Timothy not as an assistant but as a brother, linking their ministries through shared suffering and shared joy.

The Church has always been a fellowship of freed prisoners—men and women redeemed from bondage, sent out to strengthen others. The mention of Timothy's release is a whisper of hope: deliverance still happens, God still opens doors, and His servants still labor side by side for the gospel.

The Salutation of Love

"Salute all them that have the rule over you, and all the saints." These final greetings restore the family tone that runs beneath the entire letter. The writer has warned, reasoned, and wept—but now he simply embraces. The leaders and the saints are greeted together, reminding us that hierarchy has no place in heaven's family. Those who guide and those who follow are bound by the same grace and share the same inheritance.

"They of Italy salute you." A simple line, but it hints at the global reach of the gospel. From Jerusalem to Italy, from persecution to praise, the message of Christ's supremacy had crossed every boundary. Geography and government could not divide the people of God. Their unity was not political but personal—anchored in the blood of the everlasting covenant.

The Final Benediction

"Grace be with you all. Amen." The letter that began with majesty—"God, who at sundry times and in divers manners spake in time past unto the fathers by the prophets..."—ends with mercy. The first word was God; the last word is grace. Between those two words lies the whole story of redemption.

Grace is the atmosphere of the unshakable kingdom. It is the air the saints breathe, the ground they walk, the promise that sustains their perseverance. Every warning of Hebrews, every command, every example finds its fulfillment here: grace to endure, grace to obey, grace to finish.

The Farewell of Love

The final Amen is not a period but a pulse. It echoes through every generation of believers who read this letter and find strength to keep going. The same grace that called the Hebrews to stand firm still calls us today—to live as citizens of a kingdom that cannot be moved, to fix our eyes on the unchanging Christ, and to bear His reproach with joy.

The unshakable kingdom has one anthem, one foundation, one future—and one King. He is the same yesterday, today, and forever. His grace abides. His covenant stands. His people endure.

Grace be with you all.

Amen.

Summary

Hebrews 13 gathers all the threads of the book into a single tapestry: love—steadfast, sacrificial, sanctifying love. The letter that began with the glory of Christ enthroned ends with the grace of Christ expressed. The unshakable kingdom is not upheld by angels, rituals, or ceremonies, but by hearts transformed through faith and love.

Brotherly love continues because it is rooted in eternity. It is not mere affection but action—hospitality that opens its doors, empathy that remembers the suffering, fidelity that honors marriage, contentment that trusts God's providence, and generosity that shares without seeking return. Such love is more than sentiment; it is sanctified behavior.

Love obeys, submits, and serves—not under compulsion, but from gratitude. It listens to shepherds, not as lords, but as watchmen who bear responsibility for souls. Love endures reproach with Christ outside the camp, knowing that we have no continuing city here, but we seek one to come. Love worships continually, offering the sacrifice of praise— the fruit of lips that confess His name.

And when love has finished working, it still worships. The final benediction draws all glory back to the Shepherd who died and rose again. The peace that began the covenant now perfects it. God Himself works in us that which is well-pleasing in His sight. The letter closes with grace—the same grace that saved, sustained, and sanctified every generation of saints.

The faith that endures becomes hope that rejoices;

and hope that rejoices becomes love that remains.

Application

- **Continue in Brotherly Love:** Do not let affection grow cold or fellowship fade. Love is not a mood but a mission. Keep your heart open to strangers, your hands open to those in need, and your eyes open to those who hurt.

- **Honor Marriage and Purity:** Guard the sacred covenant of marriage. Let fidelity be your testimony and purity your worship. The holy life is not a restriction but a reflection of God's holiness.

- **Live Content and Dependent:** Refuse envy. Be grateful for what you have. God's promise—"I will never leave thee nor forsake thee"—is wealth enough. Rest in His providence, not your possessions.

- **Stand Firm in Grace:** Anchor your heart in the unchanging gospel. Do not chase novelty or drift into speculation. Grace is the unshakable center of the Christian life. Let your heart be established there.

- **Bear Reproach Willingly:** Go outside the camp with Christ. Do not seek the approval of the world or the comfort of conformity. Love that is unashamed of Jesus will never be unremembered by Him.

- **Seek the City to Come:** Live as a pilgrim, not a settler. Hold lightly what fades and hold firmly what lasts. The eternal city is already being built in your obedience.

- **Offer the Sacrifice of Praise:** Worship continually—when the sun shines and when shadows fall. Let thanksgiving and generosity mark your daily life. These are the sacrifices in which God delights.

- **Honor God's Order in the Church:** Respect those who watch for your souls, and make their work a joy, not a grief. Unity in the body magnifies the Shepherd of the flock.

- **Live Under the Benediction of Grace:** Remember that the Shepherd who bled for you now works in you. Let His peace steady your heart, His purpose shape your actions, and His glory be your aim.

The mark of an unshakable life is not strength, but surrender—

not pride, but peace—

not fear, but love.

Prayer

Our Father,
We thank You for the kingdom that cannot be moved, for the Shepherd who cannot fail, and for the covenant that cannot fade.
Teach us to let brotherly love continue— to see in every soul a neighbor, in every burden a

calling, and in every reproach a share in
Christ's cross.
Establish our hearts with grace. Keep us from
the pride of novelty and the fear of loss. Let
the sacrifice of praise rise daily from our lips,
and the fruit of good works spring from our
lives.
Make us content in Your providence, faithful in
Your service, and joyful in Your peace.
Perfect us in every good work to do Your will,
working in us that which is well-pleasing in
Your sight—
through Jesus Christ our Lord,
with the Spirit, in whose power we walk,
and in the name of Jesus, our great
Shepherd.
Amen.

Epilogue — The Kingdom That Remains

When the book of Hebrews ends, nothing is left for us to build—only to believe, and to behold. Every altar has been cleared, every priesthood eclipsed, every shadow dissolved in the brightness of Christ. The mountain still shakes, but the kingdom still stands.

The unshakable kingdom is not a place we will one day enter; it is a life already begun in those who belong to the Son. Its citizens are the broken made whole, the wanderers brought home, the servants who look up and find their labor woven into eternity. Faith is their language, obedience their culture, love their law. Their anthem is grace.

Each page of this letter has brought us closer to that reality—from the throne of the exalted Christ to the trembling foot of Mount Zion; from the altar of blood to the city of the living God. Its message is as steady as it is urgent: Do not drift. Do not draw back. Do not let go. For the same hand that shook the heavens still upholds the world by the word of His power.

When your world feels fragile, remember: what God shakes, He never breaks. The shaking loosens the temporary so that the eternal may stand revealed. The purpose of every trial is not your ruin but your rooting—to fix you more firmly in the unchanging Christ.

So let us go on. Let us bear His reproach outside the camp, counting it joy to belong to Him. Let us love as those who have been loved, serve as those who have been saved, and worship as those who have already crossed the threshold of glory. And when the last trumpet sounds, we will not be moved, for the kingdom will already be ours.

"Wherefore we receiving a kingdom which cannot be moved, let us have grace, whereby we may serve God acceptably with reverence and godly fear." — Hebrews 12:28

Grace be with you all. Amen.

Glossary

Aorist Tense

A Greek verb form describing an action viewed as complete and whole — emphasizing the fact of the action rather than its duration. Often used to describe Christ's finished work on the cross (Heb. 1:3).

Archēgos

Greek for captain, pioneer, or originator. Used in Hebrews 2:10 to describe Christ as the Captain of salvation, the One who goes before and brings His people safely through.

Covenant

A binding agreement established by God. In Hebrews, the Old Covenant points to shadows of sacrifice, while the New Covenant fulfills them through the once-for-all work of Christ (Heb. 8–10).

Charaktēr

Greek for engraving or impress. Translated "express image" (Heb. 1:3). Portrays Jesus as the perfect imprint of the Father's nature—the visible stamp of the invisible God.

Eschaton / Last Days

The final period in God's redemptive plan, inaugurated by Christ's death, resurrection, and ascension. In Hebrews, "these last days" (1:2) describes our current age—the final era before His return.

Faith

Trust in the unseen reality of God's promise, expressed in obedience. Hebrews 11 defines it as "the substance of things hoped for, the evidence of things not seen."

High Priest

One appointed to represent man before God through sacrifice. Jesus is the eternal High Priest, sinless and seated at God's right hand, whose single offering perfects forever those who believe (Heb. 7–10).

Hypostasis

Greek for substance or essence. In Hebrews 1:3 it denotes the real nature of God. The Son is the perfect manifestation of that divine essence.

Incarnation

The act of God the Son taking on human flesh in the person of Jesus Christ (John 1:14). Central to Hebrews' portrayal of the Savior who shares our nature yet remains without sin (Heb. 2:14–18; 4:15).

Klēronomos / Inheritance

Greek term for heir. Christ is "appointed heir of all things" (Heb. 1:2), and believers are made co-heirs with Him (Rom. 8:17). Denotes possession of all that the Son has secured.

Law

The Mosaic covenant's commands and rituals. Hebrews shows the Law as a shadow of the good things to come (Heb. 10:1), fulfilled and surpassed in Christ.

Majesty on High

A reverent title for God the Father, emphasizing His sovereign glory (Heb. 1:3). Christ's exaltation to the right hand of this Majesty declares His completed work and divine status.

Mediator

Not a negotiator between equals, but the medium of atonement—the Person through whom reconciliation is accomplished. Jesus is "the mediator of a better covenant" (Heb. 8:6).

Midrash

A Jewish interpretive method that expands or applies Scripture through stories, analogies, and moral insights. Hebrews employs midrashic exposition to reveal how the Old Testament finds its fulfillment in Christ.

Orthodoxy

A term meaning "right belief." It refers to holding sound, biblically faithful doctrine about God, Christ, and salvation. Orthodoxy guards truth from distortion and anchors the church's teaching in divine revelation. In Hebrews, orthodoxy centers on the supremacy and sufficiency of Christ, through whom God has spoken fully and finally (Heb. 1:1–2). True orthodoxy naturally leads to orthopraxy—right living shaped by right belief.

Orthopraxy

A term meaning "right practice." In Scripture, true faith produces right living—belief expressed through obedience. Orthopraxy complements orthodoxy (right belief); together they describe the harmony of doctrine and deed. Hebrews repeatedly joins these, calling believers not only to hold truth firmly but to live it faithfully (Heb. 10:23–24).

Parousia

Greek for presence or coming. Refers to Christ's future visible return in glory (Heb. 9:28).

Priesthood

The divinely appointed system of sacrifice and intercession. The Levitical priesthood served as a type pointing to the superior, eternal priesthood of Christ after the order of Melchizedek (Heb. 7).

Purification

The cleansing of sin through sacrifice. Hebrews contrasts the repetitive cleansing of the old system with the once-for-all purification accomplished by Christ (Heb. 1:3; 9:14).

Revelation

God's act of self-disclosure. In former times He spoke through prophets; in these last days He has spoken fully and finally in His Son (Heb. 1:1–2).

Sabbath Rest

The spiritual rest found in trusting Christ's finished work. Believers "enter into rest" not by ceasing labor alone, but by ceasing from self-righteous striving (Heb. 4:9–10).

Shadow and Substance

Old Covenant forms (temple, priesthood, sacrifices) are shadows that prefigure the substance found in Christ (Heb. 8:5; 10:1).

Teleioō

Greek verb meaning to make complete or bring to fulfillment. Used of Christ's mission being perfected through suffering (Heb. 2:10; 5:9)—not moral improvement, but mission accomplished.

The Three Classes of Hearers

A pastoral lens for reading Hebrews:

1.   Believers (the anchored),

2.   Admirers (the intrigued but undecided),

3.   Resisters (the hardened).

Each section of the epistle—and of this commentary—addresses these three in turn.

Throne of Grace

Symbol of divine access secured by Christ's priestly work. Believers may "come boldly unto the throne of grace" (Heb. 4:16) to find mercy and help.

Word of His Power

The sustaining and creative command of Christ (Heb. 1:3). His spoken Word not only brought creation into being but continues to uphold it and direct it toward redemption's goal.

Bibliography

Attridge, Harold W. *The Epistle to the Hebrews.* Hermeneia. Philadelphia: Fortress Press, 1989.

Black, David Alan. *Origen on the Authorship of Hebrews.* Dave Black Online, February 5, 2004. https://www.daveblackonline.com/origen_on_the_authorship_of_hebr.htm..

Blynov, David. *Who Authored the Letter to the Hebrews?* Medium, December 11, 2023. https://medium.com/@davidblynov/who-authored_the-letter-to-the-hebrews-267dae68a044.

Boyd, Rick. "The Role of Hebrews 1:1–4 in the Book of Hebrews." *Journal of Inductive Biblical Studies 2*, no. 1 (2015): 1–15.

Caird, G. B. "The Exegetical Method of the Epistle to the Hebrews." *Journal of Theological Studies 5*, no. 2 (1954): 44–51. (Reprinted in Just Men Made Perfect, 1976.)

deSilva, David A. *Perseverance in Gratitude: A Socio-Rhetorical Commentary on the Epistle "to the Hebrews."* Grand Rapids: Eerdmans, 2000.

Ellingworth, Paul. *The New International Greek Testament Commentary: The Epistle to the Hebrews.* Grand Rapids: Eerdmans, 1993.

Guthrie, George H. Hebrews: *The NIV Application Commentary.* Grand Rapids: Zondervan, 1998.

Guzik, David. *"Enduring Word Bible Commentary: Hebrews Chapter 1."* Enduring Word, 2015. https://enduringword.com/bible-commentary/hebrews-1/.

Hagner, Donald A. *Hebrews: A Good Start.* Louisville: Westminster John Knox, 2002.

Hurst, L. D. "The Christology of Hebrews 1 and 2." In *The Epistle to the Hebrews and Christian Theology,* edited by Richard Bauckham et al., 151–57. Grand Rapids: Eerdmans, 1990.

Koester, Craig R. Hebrews: *A New Translation with Introduction and Commentary.* Anchor Bible. New York: Doubleday, 2001.

Lane, William L. Hebrews 1–8. Vol. 47A, *Word Biblical Commentary.* Dallas: Word, 1991.

Mitchell, Alan C. *Hebrews.* Sacra Pagina. Collegeville, MN: Liturgical Press, 2007.

Mohler, Albert. "Hebrews 1:1-4." AlbertMohler.com, August 22, 2010. https://albertmohler.com/2010/08/22/hebrews-11-4/.

O'Brien, Peter T. *The Letter to the Hebrews. Pillar New Testament Commentary.* Grand Rapids: Eerdmans, 2010.

Origen. *Commentary on Romans* (fragments). Translated by Thomas P. Scheck. Washington, DC: Catholic University of America Press, 2009.

Third Millennium Ministries. "The Genre of Hebrews." Accessed October 21, 2025. https://thirdmill.org/answers/answer.asp/file/43288.

Thompson, James W. *Hebrews: A Commentary.* Louisville: Westminster John Knox, 2008.

Zondervan Academic. *Who Wrote the Book of Hebrews?* April 17, 2017. https://zondervanacademic.com/blog/who-wrote-the-book-of-hebrews.

About the Author

James Burke is the senior pastor of Grace Community Church in Marinette, Wisconsin. With a passion for preaching God's Word and shepherding God's people, he has spent decades helping believers grow in faith and guiding churches toward gospel-centered health. His ministry is marked by a commitment to Scripture, a love for Christ's church, and a desire to see lives transformed by the power of the cross. When he isn't preaching or writing, James enjoys time with his wife Roxanne, meaningful conversations over coffee, and the beauty of life along the shores of Lake Michigan.